C. S. Lewis has been called "one of the most influential spokesmen for Christianity in the English-speaking world." Over the years, literally millions of readers have found *Mere Christianity* to be their personal key to a life-changing faith. Lewis speaks clearly to his readers on the beliefs of Christianity—the most common and basic building-blocks of the faith itself.

"It is the book God has used
most powerfully in my life,
apart from His own Word."

FROM THE INTRODUCTION
BY CHARLES W. COLSON

THE CHRISTIAN LIBRARY has been designed and produced for the discerning book lover. These classics of the Christian faith have been printed and bound with beauty, readability and longevity in mind. Greatest care has gone into the selection of these volumes, with the hope that you will not only find books that are a joy to read, but books that will stir your faith and enlighten your daily walk with the Lord.

Books available include:

ABIDE IN CHRIST, Andrew Murray
ABSOLUTE SURRENDER, Andrew Murray
BEN-HUR: A TALE OF THE CHRIST, Lew Wallace
THE CHRISTIAN'S SECRET OF A HAPPY LIFE,
Hannah Whitall Smith
THE CONFESSIONS OF ST. AUGUSTINE
DAILY LIGHT
EACH NEW DAY, Corrie ten Boom
FOXE'S CHRISTIAN MARTYRS OF THE WORLD
GOD CALLING, A.J. Russell
THE GOD OF ALL COMFORT, Hannah Whitall Smith
THE IMITATION OF CHRIST, Thomas a Kempis
IN HIS STEPS, Charles M. Sheldon
MERE CHRISTIANITY, C.S. Lewis
THE PILGRIM'S PROGRESS, John Bunyan
POWER THROUGH PRAYER/
PURPOSE IN PRAYER, E.M. Bounds
QUIET TALKS ON PRAYER, S.D. Gordon

MERE CHRISTIANITY

AN ANNIVERSARY EDITION OF THE THREE BOOKS

The Case for Christianity, Christian Behaviour,
and
Beyond Personality

BY

C. S. LEWIS

Complete and Unabridged

Barbour and Company, Inc.
164 Mill Street
Westwood, New Jersey

This edition is reprinted by arrangement with Macmillan Publishing Company, a Division of Macmillan, Inc.

ISBN 0-916441-18-0
(Canadian ISBN 0-920413-09-9)

Published by: **BARBOUR AND COMPANY, INC.**
164 Mill Street
Westwood, New Jersey 07675

(In Canada, THE CHRISTIAN LIBRARY,
960 The Gateway, Burlington, Ontario L7L 5K7)

Printed in the United States of America

INTRODUCTION
Charles W. Colson

One hot summer night in August of 1973 I visited an old friend at his home outside of Boston. It was during the darkest days of Watergate. My whole world was being turned upside down.

My friend was a keen businessman who had worked his way to the top. President of one of the largest corporations in America in his early forties, he was a hard-charging man driven to succeed. I understood—I was just like him.

But when I had paid him a quick visit during a business trip several months earlier, I had been astonished to find him peaceful, calm, relaxed: dramatically different.

When I asked him about it, he answered with an extraordinary explanation: "I have accepted Jesus Christ." I had never heard anything like those words before; but I could not deny he had changed.

So, this August night, though I couldn't admit it to anyone, I was seeking something—and I knew my friend might have an answer. Something was wrong in my own life. Something much more than Watergate; I was empty inside, groping for whatever meaning there was to life, if indeed there was any.

That night he told me about his encounter with Jesus Christ, how his life had been transformed. Then he picked up a book off a coffee table, opened it to a chapter titled "Pride" and began to read.

It was one of the most extraordinary moments of my life. The words from that book—*Mere Christianity*, written by the great English scholar C.S. Lewis—ripped through the protective armor in which I had unknowingly encased myself for forty-one years. Lewis wrote about man's great sin—his pride—as a spiritual cancer.

The events of my own life flashed before me. I thought I had been driven by a desire to provide for my family, build a good law firm, serve my country. But in reality what I was doing all those years was feeding my pride, proving how good I was. Lewis convicted me that all my efforts had been in vain, that in my drive for the top I had missed the real pinnacle—to know God in a personal way.

As I left my friend's home that night, I accepted his gift of the copy of *Mere Christianity*. I was deeply moved by his testimony and by the chapter he had read—though I refused to show it. But as I got into my car, the White House tough guy— the hatchet-man, or so the press called me—crumbled in a flood of tears, unable to drive, calling out to God with the first honest prayer of my life. That was the night Jesus Christ came into my life.

Over the next week I studied *Mere Christianity*. I underlined, made notes, even kept a yellow pad at my side with two columns—one headed "there is a God," the other headed "there is not a God." On another sheet of paper I had two more columns—"Jesus Christ is God"—"Jesus Christ is not God."

I read the book as if I was studying for the most important case I had ever argued. Lewis' logic was so utterly compelling that I was left with no recourse but to accept the reality of the God Who is and Who has revealed Himself through Jesus Christ. *Mere Christianity* simply sets forth a powerful, rational case for the Christian faith in a wonderfully readable way.

Since then I have given out hundreds of copies of *Mere Christianity* and have met thousands whose lives have been transformed by it. It is the book God has used most powerfully in my life, apart from His own Word.

But I must warn you, it is not a book you can pick up and put down easily, nor is it a book you can read and return to being the same person you were before. For it masterfully presents the case for Christ. After reading it, the uncommitted person can only make a choice for or against Him. In the choice for Him, the reader will discover, as did Lewis himself in his own conversion, that "the hardness of God is kinder than the softness of man, and His compulsion is our liberation."

Contents

Contents

Book IV.

Beyond Personality: or First Steps in the Doctrine of the Trinity

Preface

THE CONTENTS OF THIS BOOK were first given on the air, and then published in three separate parts as *The Case for Christianity* (1943),* *Christian Behaviour* (1943) and *Beyond Personality* (1945). In the printed versions I made a few additions to what I had said at the microphone, but otherwise left the text much as it had been. A "talk" on the radio should, I think, be as like real talk as possible, and should not sound like an essay being read aloud. In my talks I had therefore used all the contractions and colloquialisms I ordinarily use in conversation. In the printed version I reproduced this, putting *don't* and *we've* for *do not* and *we have*. And wherever, in the talks, I had made the importance of a word clear by the emphasis of my voice, I printed it in italics. I am now inclined to think that this was a mistake—an undesirable hybrid between the art of speaking and the art of writing. A talker ought to use variations of voice for emphasis because his medium naturally lends itself to that method: but a writer ought not to use italics for the same purpose. He has his own, different, means of bringing out the key words and ought to use them. In this edition I have expanded the contractions and replaced most of

*Published in England under the title *Broadcast Talks*.

the italics by recasting the sentences in which they occurred: but without altering, I hope, the "popular" or "familiar" tone which I had all along intended. I have also added and deleted where I thought I understood any part of my subject better now than ten years ago or where I knew that the original version had been misunderstood by others.

The reader should be warned that I offer no help to anyone who is hesitating between two Christian "denominations." You will not learn from me whether you ought to become an Anglican, a Methodist, a Presbyterian, or a Roman Catholic. This omission is intentional (even in the list I have just given the order is alphabetical). There is no mystery about my own position. I am a very ordinary layman of the Church of England, not especially "high," nor especially "low," nor especially anything else. But in this book I am not trying to convert anyone to my own position. Ever since I became a Christian I have thought that the best, perhaps the only, service I could do for my unbelieving neighbours was to explain and defend the belief that has been common to nearly all Christians at all times. I had more than one reason for thinking this. In the first place, the questions which divide Christians from one another often involve points of high Theology or even of ecclesiastical history which ought never to be treated except by real experts. I should have been out of my depth in such waters: more in need of help myself than able to help others. And secondly, I think we must admit that the discussion of these disputed points has no tendency at all to bring an outsider into the Christian fold. So long as we write and talk about them we are much more likely to deter him from entering any Christian communion than to draw him into our own. Our divisions should never be discussed except in the presence of those who have already come to believe that there is one God and that Jesus Christ is His only Son. Finally, I got the impression that far more, and more talented, authors were already engaged in such controversial matters than in the defence of what Baxter calls "mere" Christianity. That part of the line where I thought I could serve best was also the part that seemed to be thinnest. And to it I naturally went.

So far as I know, these were my only motives, and I should be very glad if people would not draw fanciful inferences from my silence on certain disputed matters.

For example, such silence need not mean that I myself am sitting on the fence. Sometimes I am. There are questions at issue between Christians to which I do not think I have the answer. There are some to which I may never know the answer: if I asked them, even in a better world, I might (for all I know) be answered as a far greater questioner was answered: "What is that to thee? Follow thou Me." But there are other questions as to which I am definitely on one side of the fence, and yet say nothing. For I was not writing to expound something I could call "my religion," but to expound "mere" Christianity, which is what it is and was what it was long before I was born and whether I like it or not.

Some people draw unwarranted conclusions from the fact that I never say more about the Blessed Virgin Mary than is involved in asserting the Virgin Birth of Christ. But surely my reason for not doing so is obvious? To say more would take me at once into highly controversial regions. And there is no controversy between Christians which needs to be so delicately touched as this. The Roman Catholic beliefs on that subject are held not only with the ordinary fervour that attaches to all sincere religious belief, but (very naturally) with the peculiar and, as it were, chivalrous sensibility that a man feels when the honour of his mother or his beloved is at stake. It is very difficult so to dissent from them that you will not appear to them a cad as well as a heretic. And contrariwise, the opposed Protestant beliefs on this subject call forth feelings which go down to the very roots of all Monotheism whatever. To radical Protestants it seems that the distinction between Creator and creature (however holy) is imperilled: that Polytheism is risen again. Hence it is hard so to dissent from them that you will not appear something worse than a heretic—an idolator, a Pagan. If any topic could be relied upon to wreck a book about "mere" Christianity—if any topic makes utterly unprofitable reading for those who do not yet believe that the Virgin's son is God—surely this is it.

Oddly enough, you cannot even conclude, from my silence on disputed points, either that I think them important or that I think them unimportant. For this is itself one of the disputed points. One of the things Christians are disagreed about is the importance of their disagreements. When two Christians of different denominations start arguing, it is usually not long before one asks whether such-and-such a point "really matters" and the other replies: "Matter? Why, it's absolutely essential."

All this is said simply in order to make clear what kind of book I was trying to write; not in the least to conceal or evade responsibility for my own beliefs. About those, as I said before, there is no secret. To quote Uncle Toby: "They are written in the Common-Prayer Book."

The danger clearly was that I should put forward as common Christianity anything that was peculiar to the Church of England or (worse still) to myself. I tried to guard against this by sending the original script of what is now Book II to four clergymen (Anglican, Methodist, Presbyterian, Roman Catholic) and asking for their criticism. The Methodist thought I had not said enough about Faith, and the Roman Catholic thought I had gone rather too far about the comparative unimportance of theories in explanation of the Atonement. Otherwise all five of us were agreed. I did not have the remaining books similarly "vetted" because in them, though differences might arise among Christians, these would be differences between individuals or schools of thought, not between denominations.

So far as I can judge from reviews and from the numerous letters written to me, the book, however faulty in other respects, did at least succeed in presenting an agreed, or common, or central, or "mere" Christianity. In that way it may possibly be of some help in silencing the view that, if we omit the disputed points, we shall have left only a vague and blood-less H.C.F. The H.C.F. turns out to be something not only positive but pungent; divided from all non-Christian beliefs by a chasm to which the worst divisions inside Christendom are not really comparable at all. If I have not directly helped the cause of reunion, I have perhaps made it clear why we ought to be reunited. Certainly I have met with little of the fabled *odium theologicum* from convinced members of com-munions different from my own. Hostility has come more from borderline people whether within the Church of England or without it: men not exactly obedient to any communion. This I find curiously consoling. It is at her centre, where her truest children dwell, that each communion is really closest to every other in spirit, if not in doctrine. And this suggests that at the centre of each there is something, or a Someone, who against all divergences of belief, all differences of tempera-ment, all memories of mutual persecution, speaks with the same voice.

So much for my omissions on doctrine. In Book III, which deals with morals, I have also passed over some things in si-lence, but for a different reason. Ever since I served as an in-fantryman in the first world war I have had a great dislike of people who, themselves in ease and safety, issue exhortations to men in the front line. As a result I have a reluctance to say much about temptations to which I myself am not exposed. No man, I suppose, is tempted to every sin. It so happens that the impulse which makes men gamble has been left out of my make-up; and, no doubt, I pay for this by lacking some good impulse of which it is the excess or perversion. I therefore did not feel myself qualified to give advice about permissable and impermissable gambling: if there is any permissable, for I do not claim to know even that. I have also said nothing about birth-control. I am not a woman nor even a married man, nor am I a priest. I did not think it my place to take a firm line about pains, dangers and expenses from which I am protected; having no pastoral office which obliged me to do so.

Far deeper objections may be felt—and have been expressed—against my use of the word *Christian* to mean one who accepts the common doctrines of Christianity. People ask: "Who are you, to lay down who is, and who is not a Christian?" or "May not many a man who cannot believe these doctrines be far more truly a Christian, far closer to the spirit of Christ, than some who do?" Now this objection is in one sense very right, very charitable, very spiritual, very sensitive. It has every amiable quality except that of being useful. We simply cannot, without disaster, use language as these objectors want us to use it. I will try to make this clear by the history of another, and very much less important, word.

The word *gentleman* originally meant something recognisable; one who had a coat of arms and some landed property. When you called someone "a gentleman" you were not paying him a compliment, but merely stating a fact. If you said he was not "a gentleman" you were not insulting him, but giving information. There was no contradiction in saying that John was a liar and a gentleman; any more than there now is in saying that James is a fool and an M.A. But then there came people who said—so rightly, charitably, spiritually, sensitively, so anything but usefully—"Ah, but surely the important thing about a gentleman is not the coat of arms and the land, but the behaviour? Surely he is the true gentleman who behaves as a gentleman should? Surely in that sense Edward is far more truly a gentleman than John?" They meant well. To be honourable and courteous and brave is of course a far better thing than to have a coat of arms. But it is not the same thing. Worse still, it is not a thing everyone will agree about. To call a man "a gentleman" in this new, refined sense, becomes, in fact, not a way of giving information about him, but a way of praising him: to deny that he is "a gentleman" becomes simply a way of insulting him. When a word ceases to be a term of description and becomes merely a term of praise, it no longer tells you facts about the object: it only tells you about the speaker's attitude to that object. (A "nice" meal only means a meal the speaker likes.) A *gentleman*, once it has been spiritualised and refined out of its old coarse, objective sense, means hardly more than a man whom the speaker likes. As a result, *gentleman* is now a useless word. We had lots of terms of approval already, so it was not needed for that use; on the other hand if anyone (say, in a historical work) wants to use it in its old sense, he cannot do so without explanations. It has been spoiled for that purpose.

Now if once we allow people to start spiritualising and refining, or as they might say "deepening," the sense of the word *Christian*, it too will speedily become a useless word. In the first place, Christians themselves will never be able to apply it to anyone. It is not for us to say who, in the deepest sense, is or is not close to the spirit of Christ. We do not see into men's hearts. We cannot judge, and are indeed forbidden to judge. It would be wicked arrogance for us to say that any man is, or is not, a Christian in this refined sense. And obviously a word which we can never apply is not going to be a very useful word. As for the unbelievers, they will no doubt cheerfully use the word in the refined sense. It will become in their mouths simply a term of praise. In calling anyone a Christian they will mean that they think him a good man. But that way of using the word will be no enrichment of the language, for we already have the word *good*. Meanwhile, the word *Christian* will have been spoiled for any really useful purpose it might have served.

We must therefore stick to the original, obvious meaning. The name *Christians* was first given at Antioch (Acts xi. 26) to "the disciples," to those who accepted the teaching of the apostles. There is no question of its being restricted to those who profited by that teaching as much as they should have. There is no question of its being extended to those who in some refined, spiritual, inward fashion were "far closer to the spirit of Christ" than the less satisfactory of the disciples. The point is not a theological, or moral one. It is only a question of using words so that we can all understand what is being said. When a man who accepts the Christian doctrine lives unworthily of it, it is much clearer to say he is a bad Christian than to say he is not a Christian.

I hope no reader will suppose that "mere" Christianity is here put forward as an alternative to the creeds of the existing communions—as if a man could adopt it in preference to Congregationalism or Greek Orthodoxy or anything else. It is more like a hall out of which doors open into several rooms. If I can bring anyone into that hall I shall have done what I attempted. But it is in the rooms, not in the hall, that there are fires and chairs and meals. The hall is a place to wait in, a place from which to try the various doors, not a place to live in. For that purpose the worst of the rooms (whichever that may be) is, I think, preferable. It is true that some people may find they have to wait in the hall for a considerable time, while others feel certain almost at once which door they must knock at. I do not know why there is this difference, but I am sure God keeps no one waiting unless He sees that it is good for him to wait. When you do get into your room you will find that the long wait has done you some kind of good which you would not have had otherwise. But you must regard it as waiting, not as camping. You must keep on praying for light: and, of course, even in the hall, you must begin trying to obey the rules which are common to the whole house. And above all you must be asking which door is the true one; not which pleases you best by its paint and panelling. In plain language, the question should never be: "Do I like that kind of service?" but "Are these doctrines true: Is holiness here? Does my conscience move me towards this? Is my reluctance to knock at this door due to my pride, or my mere taste, or my personal dislike of this particular door-keeper?"

When you have reached your own room, be kind to those who have chosen different doors and to those who are still in the hall. If they are wrong they need your prayers all the more; and if they are your enemies, then you are under orders to pray for them. That is one of the rules common to the whole house.

BOOK I

---

*Right and Wrong as a Clue to
the Meaning of the Universe*

CHAPTER 1

The Law of Human Nature

Every one has heard people quarrelling. Sometimes it sounds funny and sometimes it sounds merely unpleasant; but however it sounds, I believe we can learn something very important from listening to the kind of things they say. They say things like this: "How'd you like it if anyone did the same to you?"—"That's my seat, I was there first"—"Leave him alone, he isn't doing you any harm"—"Why should you shove in first?"—"Give me a bit of your orange, I gave you a bit of mine"—"Come on, you promised." People say things like that every day, educated people as well as uneducated, and children as well as grown-ups.

Now what interests me about all these remarks is that the man who makes them is not merely saying that the other man's behaviour does not happen to please him. He is appealing to some kind of standard of behaviour which he expects the other man to know about. And the other man very seldom replies: "To hell with your standard." Nearly always he tries to make out that what he has been doing does not really go against the standard, or that if it does there is some special excuse. He pretends there is some special reason in this particular case why the person who took the seat first should not keep it, or that things were quite different when he was given the bit of orange, or that something has turned up which lets him off keeping his promise. It looks, in fact, very much as if both parties had in mind some kind of Law or Rule of fair play or decent behaviour or morality or whatever you like to call it, about which they really agreed. And they have. If they had not, they might, of course, fight like animals, but they could not *quarrel* in the human sense of the word. Quarrelling means trying to show that the other man is in the wrong. And there would be no sense in trying to do that unless you and he had some sort of agreement as to what Right and Wrong are; just as there would be no sense in saying that a footballer had committed a foul unless there was some agreement about the rules of football.

Now this Law or Rule about Right and Wrong used to be called the Law of Nature. Nowadays, when we talk of the "laws of nature" we usually mean things like gravitation, or heredity, or the laws of chemistry. But when the older thinkers called the Law of Right and Wrong "the Law of Nature," they really meant the Law of *Human* Nature. The idea was that, just as all bodies are governed by the law of gravitation and organisms by biological laws, so the creature called man also has *his* law—with this great difference, that a body could not choose whether it obeyed the law of gravitation or not, but a man could choose either to obey the Law of Human Nature or to disobey it.

We may put this another way. Each man is at every moment subjected to several different sets of law but there is only one of these which he is free to disobey. As a body, he is subjected to gravitation and cannot disobey it; if you leave him unsupported in mid-air, he has no more choice about falling than a stone has. As an organism, he is subjected to various biological laws which he cannot disobey any more than an animal can. That is, he cannot disobey those laws which he shares with other things; but the law which is peculiar to his human nature, the law he does not share with animals or vegetables or inorganic things, is the one he can disobey if he chooses.

This law was called the Law of Nature because people thought that every one knew it by nature and did not need to be taught it. They did not mean, of course, that you might not find an odd individual here and there who did not know it, just as you find a few people who are colour-blind or have no ear for a tune. But taking the race as a whole, they thought that the human idea of decent behaviour was obvious to every one. And I believe they were right. If they were not, then all the things we said about the war were nonsense. What was the sense in saying the enemy were in the wrong unless Right is a real thing which the Nazis at bottom knew as well as we did and ought to have practised? If they had had no notion of what we mean by right, then, though we might still have had to fight them, we could no more have blamed them for that than for the colour of their hair.

I know that some people say the idea of a Law of Nature or decent behaviour known to all men is unsound, because different civilisations and different ages have had quite different moralities.

But this is not true. There have been differences between their moralities, but these have never amounted to anything like a total difference. If anyone will take the trouble to compare the moral teaching of, say, the ancient Egyptians, Babylonians, Hindus, Chinese, Greeks and Romans, what will really strike him will be how very like they are to each other and to our own. Some of the evidence for this I have put together in the appendix of another book called *The Abolition of Man;* but for our present purpose I need only ask the reader to think what a totally different morality would mean. Think of a country where people were admired for running away in battle, or where a man felt proud of double-crossing all the people who had been kindest to him. You might just as well try to imagine a country where two and two made five. Men have differed as regards what people you ought to be unselfish to—whether it was only your own family, or your fellow countrymen, or everyone. But they have always agreed that you ought not to put yourself first. Selfishness has never been admired. Men have differed as to whether you should have one wife or four. But they have always agreed that you must not simply have any woman you liked.

But the most remarkable thing is this. Whenever you find a man who says he does not believe in a real Right and Wrong, you will find the same man going back on this a moment later. He may break his promise to you, but if you try breaking one to him he will be complaining "It's not fair" before you can say Jack Robinson. A nation may say treaties do not matter; but then, next minute, they spoil their case by saying that the particular treaty they want to break was an unfair one. But if treaties do not matter, and if there is no such thing as Right and Wrong—in other words, if there is no Law of Nature—what is the difference between a fair treaty and an unfair one? Have they not let the cat out of the bag and shown that, whatever they say, they really know the Law of Nature just like anyone else?

It seems, then, we are forced to believe in a real Right and Wrong. People may be sometimes mistaken about them, just as people sometimes get their sums wrong; but they are not a matter of mere taste and opinion any more than the multiplication table. Now if we are agreed about that, I go on to my next point, which is this. None of us are really keeping the Law of Nature. If there are any exceptions among you, I apologise to them. They had much better read some other work, for nothing I am going to say concerns them. And now, turning to the ordinary human beings who are left:

I hope you will not misunderstand what I am going to say. I am not preaching, and Heaven knows I do not pretend to be better than anyone else. I am only trying to call attention to a fact; the fact that this year, or this month, or, more likely, this very day, we have failed to practise ourselves the kind of behaviour we expect from other people. There may be all sorts of excuses for us. That time you were so unfair to the children was when you were very tired. That slightly shady business about the money—the one you have almost forgotten—came when you were very hard up. And what you promised to do for old So-and-so and have never done—well, you never would have promised if you had known how frightfully busy you were going to be. And as for your behaviour to your wife (or husband) or sister (or brother) if I knew how irritating they could be, I would not wonder at it—and who the dickens am I, anyway? I am just the same. That is to say, I do not succeed in keeping the Law of Nature very well, and the moment anyone tells me I am not keeping it, there starts up in my mind a string of excuses as long as your arm. The question at the moment is not whether they are good excuses. The point is that they are one more proof of how deeply, whether we like it or not, we believe in the Law of Nature. If we do not believe in decent behaviour, why should we be so anxious to make excuses for not having behaved decently? The truth is, we believe in decency so much—we feel the Rule or Law pressing on us so—that we cannot bear to face the fact that we are breaking it, and consequently we try to shift the responsibility. For you notice that it is only for our bad behaviour that we find all these explanations. It is only our bad temper that we put down to being tired or worried or hungry; we put our good temper down to ourselves.

These, then, are the two points I wanted to make. First, that human beings, all over the earth, have this curious idea that they ought to behave in a certain way, and cannot really get rid of it. Secondly, that they do not in fact behave in that way. They know the Law of Nature; they break it. These two facts are the foundation of all clear thinking about ourselves and the universe we live in.

CHAPTER 2

Some Objections

IF THEY ARE THE FOUNDATION, I had better stop to make that foundation firm before I go on. Some of the letters I have had show that a good many people find it difficult to understand just what this Law of Human Nature, or Moral Law, or Rule of Decent Behaviour is.

For example, some people wrote to me saying, "Isn't what you call the Moral Law simply our herd instinct and hasn't it been developed just like all our other instincts?" Now I do not deny that we may have a herd instinct: but that is not what I mean by the Moral Law. We all know what it feels like to be prompted by instinct—by mother love, or sexual instinct, or the instinct for food. It means that you feel a strong want or desire to act in a certain way. And, of course, we sometimes do feel just that sort of desire to help another person: and no doubt that desire is due to the herd instinct. But feeling a desire to help is quite different from feeling that you ought to help whether you want to or not. Supposing you hear a cry for help from a man in danger. You will probably feel two desires—one a desire to give help (due to your herd instinct), the other a desire to keep out of danger (due to the instinct for self-preservation). But you will find inside you, in addition to these two impulses, a third thing which tells you that you ought to follow the impulse to help, and suppress the impulse to run away. Now this thing that judges between two instincts, that decides which should be encouraged, cannot itself be either of them. You might as well say that the sheet of music which tells you, at a given moment, to play one note on the piano and not another, is itself one of the notes on the keyboard. The Moral Law tells us the tune we have to play: our instincts are merely the keys.

Another way of seeing that the Moral Law is not simply one of our instincts is this. If two instincts are in conflict, and there is nothing in a creature's mind except those two instincts, obviously the stronger of the two must win. But at those moments when we are most conscious of the Moral Law, it usually seems to be telling us to side with the weaker of the two impulses. You probably *want* to be safe much more than you want to help the man who is drowning: but the Moral Law tells you to help him all the same. And surely it often tells us to try to make the right impulse stronger than it naturally is? I mean, we often feel it our duty to stimulate the herd instinct, by waking up our imaginations and arousing our pity and so on, so as to get up enough steam for doing the right thing. But clearly we are not acting *from* instinct when we set about making an instinct stronger than it is. The thing that says to you, "Your herd instinct is asleep. Wake it up," cannot itself *be* the herd instinct. The thing that tells you which note on the piano needs to be played louder cannot itself be that note.

Here is a third way of seeing it. If the Moral Law was one of our instincts, we ought to be able to point to some one impulse inside us which was always what we call "good," always in agreement with the rule of right behaviour. But you cannot. There is none of our impulses which the Moral Law may not sometimes tell us to suppress, and none which it may not sometimes tell us to encourage. It is a mistake to think that some of our impulses—say mother love or patriotism—are good, and others, like sex or the fighting instinct, are bad. All we mean is that the occasions on which the fighting instinct or the sexual desire need to be restrained are rather more frequent than those for restraining mother love or patriotism. But there are situations in which it is the duty of a married man to encourage his sexual impulse and of a soldier to encourage the fighting instinct. There are also occasions on which a mother's love for her own children or a man's love for his own country have to be suppressed or they will lead to unfairness towards other people's children or countries. Strictly speaking, there are no such things as good and bad impulses. Think once again of a piano. It has not got two kinds of notes on it, the "right" notes and the "wrong" ones. Every single note is right at one time and wrong at another. The Moral Law is not any one instinct or any set of instincts: it is something which makes a kind of tune (the tune we call goodness or right conduct) by directing the instincts.

By the way, this point is of great practical consequence. The most dangerous thing you can do is to take any one impulse of your own nature and set it up as the thing you ought to follow at all costs. There is not one of them which will not make us into devils if we set it up as an absolute guide. You might think love of humanity in general was safe, but it is not. If you leave out justice you will find yourself breaking agreements and faking evidence in trials "for the sake of humanity," and become in the end a cruel and treacherous man.

Other people wrote to me saying, "Isn't what you call the Moral Law just a social convention, something that is put into us by education?" I think there is a misunderstanding here. The people who ask that question are usually taking it for granted that if we have learned a thing from parents and teachers, then that thing must be merely a human invention. But, of course, that is not so. We all learned the multiplication table at school. A child who grew up alone on a desert island would not know it. But surely it does not follow that the multiplication table is simply a human convention, something human beings have made up for themselves and might have made different if they had liked? I fully agree that we learn the Rule of Decent Behaviour from parents and teachers, and friends and books, as we learn everything else. But some of the things we learn are mere conventions which might have been different—we learn to keep to the left of the road, but it might just as well have been the rule to keep to the right—and others of them, like mathematics, are real truths. The question is to which class the Law of Human Nature belongs.

There are two reasons for saying it belongs to the same class as mathematics. The first is, as I said in the first chapter, that though there are differences between the moral ideas of one time or country and those of another, the differences are not really very great—not nearly so great as most people imagine—and you can recognise the same law running through them all: whereas mere conventions, like the rule of the road or the kind of clothes people wear, may differ to any extent. The other reason is this. When you think about these differences between the morality of one people and another, do you think that the morality of one people is ever better or worse than that of another? Have any of the changes been improvements? If not, then of course there could never be any moral progress. Progress means not just changing, but changing for the better. If no set of moral ideas were truer or better than any other, there would be no sense in preferring civilised morality to savage morality, or Christian morality to Nazi morality. In fact, of course, we all do believe that some moralities are better than others. We do believe that some of the people who tried to change the moral ideas of their own age were what we would call Reformers or Pioneers—people who understood morality better than their neighbours did. Very well then. The moment you say that one set of moral ideas can be better than another, you are, in fact, measuring them both by a standard, saying that one of them conforms to that standard more nearly than the other. But the standard that measures two things is something different from either. You are, in fact, comparing them both with some Real Morality, admitting that there is such a thing as a real Right, independent of what people think, and that some people's ideas get nearer to that real Right than others. Or put it this way. If your moral ideas can be truer, and those of the Nazis less true, there must be something—some Real Morality—for them to be true about. The reason why your idea of New York can be truer or less true than mine is that New York is a real place, existing quite apart from what either of us thinks. If when each of us said "New York" each meant merely "The town I am imagining in my own head," how could one of us have truer ideas than the other? There would be no question of truth or falsehood at all. In the same way, if the Rule of Decent Behaviour meant simply "whatever each nation happens to approve," there would be no sense in saying that any one nation had ever been more correct in its approval than any other; no sense in saying that the world could ever grow morally better or morally worse.

I conclude then, that though the differences between people's ideas of Decent Behaviour often make you suspect that there is no real natural Law of Behaviour at all, yet the things we are bound to think about these differences really prove just the opposite. But one word before I end. I have met people who exaggerate the differences, because they have not distinguished between differences of morality and differences of belief about facts. For example, one man said to me, "Three hundred years ago people in England were putting witches to death. Was that what you call the Rule of Human Nature or Right Conduct?" But surely the reason we do not execute witches is that we do not believe there are such things. If we did—if we really thought that there were people going about who had sold themselves to the devil and received supernatural powers from him in return and were using these powers to kill their neighbours or drive them mad or bring bad weather, surely we would all agree that if anyone deserved the death penalty, then these filthy quislings did. There is no difference of moral principle here: the difference is simply about matter of fact. It may be a great advance in knowledge not to believe in witches: there is no moral advance in not executing them when you do not think they are there. You would not call a man humane for ceasing to set mousetraps if he did so because he believed there were no mice in the house.

CHAPTER 3
The Reality of the Law

I NOW GO BACK to what I said at the end of the first chapter, that there were two odd things about the human race. First, that they were haunted by the idea of a sort of behaviour they ought to practise, what you might call fair play, or decency, or morality, or the Law of Nature. Second, that they did not in fact do so. Now some of you may wonder why I called this odd. It may seem to you the most natural thing in the world. In particular, you may have thought I was rather hard on the human race. After all, you may say, what I call breaking the Law of Right and Wrong or of Nature, only means that people are not perfect. And why on earth should I expect them to be? That would be a good answer if what I was trying to do was to fix the exact amount of blame which is due to us for not behaving as we expect others to behave. But that is not my job at all. I am not concerned at present with blame; I am trying to find out truth. And from that point of view the very idea of something being imperfect, of its not being what it ought to be, has certain consequences.

If you take a thing like a stone or a tree, it is what it is and there seems no sense in saying it ought to have been otherwise. Of course you may say a stone is "the wrong shape" if you want to use it for a rockery, or that a tree is a bad tree because it does not give you as much shade as you expected. But all you mean is that the stone or tree does not happen to be convenient for some purpose of your own. You are not, except as a joke, blaming them for that. You really know, that, given the weather and the soil, the tree could not have been any different. What we, from our point of view, call a "bad" tree is obeying the laws of its nature just as much as a "good" one.

Now have you noticed what follows? It follows that what we usually call the laws of nature—the way weather works on a tree for example—may not really be *laws* in the strict sense, but only in a manner of speaking. When you say that falling stones always obey the law of gravitation, is not this much the same as saying that the law only means "what stones always do"? You do not really think that when a stone is let go, it suddenly remembers that it is under orders to fall to the ground. You only mean that, in fact, it does fall. In other words, you cannot be sure that there is anything over and above the facts themselves, any law about what ought to happen, as distinct from what does happen. The laws of nature, as applied to stones or trees, may only mean "what Nature, in fact, does." But if you turn to the Law of Human Nature, the Law of Decent Behaviour, it is a different matter. That law certainly does not mean "what human beings, in fact, do"; for as I said before, many of them do not obey this law at all, and none of them obey it completely. The law of gravity tells you what stones do if you drop them; but the Law of Human Nature tells you what human beings ought to do and do not. In other words, when you are dealing with humans, something else comes in above and beyond the actual facts. You have the facts (how men do behave) and you also have something else (how they ought to behave). In the rest of the universe there need not be anything but the facts. Electrons and molecules behave in a certain way, and certain results follow, and that may be the whole story.* But men behave in a certain way and

---

*I do not think it *is* the whole story, as you will see later. I mean that, as far as the argument has gone up to date, it *may* be.

that is not the whole story, for all the time you know that they ought to behave differently.

Now this is really so peculiar that one is tempted to try to explain it away. For instance, we might try to make out that when you say a man ought not to act as he does, you only mean the same as when you say that a stone is the wrong shape; namely, that what he is doing happens to be inconvenient to you. But that is simply untrue. A man occupying the corner seat in the train because he got there first, and a man who slipped into it while my back was turned and removed my bag, are both equally inconvenient. But I blame the second man and do not blame the first. I am not angry—except perhaps for a moment before I come to my senses—with a man who trips me up by accident; I am angry with a man who tries to trip me up even if he does not succeed. Yet the first has hurt me and the second has not. Sometimes the behaviour which I call bad is not inconvenient to me at all, but the very opposite. In war, each side may find a traitor on the other side very useful. But though they use him and pay him they regard him as human vermin. So you cannot say that what we call decent behaviour in others is simply the behaviour that happens to be useful to us. And as for decent behaviour in ourselves, I suppose it is pretty obvious that it does not mean the behaviour that pays. It means things like being content with thirty shillings when you might have got three pounds, doing school work honestly when it would be easy to cheat, leaving a girl alone when you would like to make love to her, staying in dangerous places when you could go somewhere safer, keeping promises you would rather not keep, and telling the truth even when it makes you look a fool.

Some people say that though decent conduct does not mean what pays each particular person at a particular moment, still, it means what pays the human race as a whole; and that consequently there is no mystery about it. Human beings, after all, have some sense; they see that you cannot have real safety or happiness except in a society where every one plays fair, and it is because they see this that they try to behave decently.

Now, of course, it is perfectly true that safety and happiness can only come from individuals, classes, and nations being honest and fair and kind to each other. It is one of the most important truths in the world. But as an explanation of why we feel as we do about Right and Wrong it just misses the point. If we ask: "Why ought I to be unselfish?" and you reply "Because it is good for society," we may then ask, "Why should I care what's good for society except when it happens to pay *me* personally?" and then you will have to say, "Because you ought to be unselfish"—which simply brings us back to where we started. You are saying what is true, but you are not getting any further. If a man asked what was the point of playing football, it would not be much good saying "in order to score goals," for trying to score goals is the game itself, not the reason for the game, and you would really only be saying that football was football—which is true, but not worth saying. In the same way, if a man asks what is the point of behaving decently, it is no good replying, "in order to benefit society," for trying to benefit society, in other words being unselfish (for "society" after all only means "other people"), is one of the things decent behaviour consists in; all you are really saying is that decent behaviour is decent behaviour. You would have said just as much if you had stopped at the statement, "Men ought to be unselfish."

And that is where I do stop. Men ought to be unselfish, ought to be fair. Not that men are unselfish, nor that they like being unselfish, but that they ought to be. The Moral Law, or Law of Human Nature, is not simply a fact about human behaviour in the same way as the Law of Gravitation is, or may be, simply a fact about how heavy objects behave. On the other hand, it is not a mere fancy, for we cannot get rid of the idea, and most of the things we say and think about men would be reduced to nonsense if we did. And it is not simply a statement about how we should like men to behave for our own convenience; for the behaviour we call bad or unfair is not exactly the same as the behaviour we find inconvenient, and may even be the opposite. Consequently, this Rule of Right and Wrong, or Law of Human Nature, or whatever you call it, must somehow or other be a real thing—a thing that is really there, not made up by ourselves. And yet it is not a fact in the ordinary sense, in the same way as our actual behaviour is a fact. It begins to look as if we shall have to admit that there is more than one kind of reality; that, in this particular case, there is something above and beyond the ordinary facts of men's behaviour, and yet quite definitely real—a real law, which none of us made, but which we find pressing on us.

CHAPTER 4

What Lies Behind the Law

L ET US SUM UP what we have reached so far. In the case of stones and trees and things of that sort, what we call the Laws of Nature may not be anything except a way of speaking. When you say that nature is governed by certain laws, this may only mean that nature does, in fact, behave in a certain way. The so-called laws may not be anything real—anything above and beyond the actual facts which we observe. But in the case of Man, we saw that this will not do. The Law of Human Nature, or of Right and Wrong, must be something above and beyond the actual facts of human behaviour. In this case, besides the actual facts, you have something else—a real law which we did not invent and which we know we ought to obey.

I now want to consider what this tells us about the universe we live in. Ever since men were able to think, they have been wondering what this universe really is and how it came to be there. And, very roughly, two views have been held. First, there is what is called the materialist view. People who take that view think that matter and space just happen to exist, and always have existed, nobody knows why; and that the matter, behaving in certain fixed ways, has just happened, by a sort of fluke, to produce creatures like ourselves who are able to think. By one chance in a thousand something hit our sun and made it produce the planets; and by another thousandth chance the chemicals necessary for life, and the right temperature, occurred on one of these planets, and so some of the matter on this earth came alive; and then, by a very long series of chances, the living creatures developed into things like us. The other view is the religious view.* According to it, what is behind the universe is more like a mind than it is like anything else we know. That is to say, it is conscious, and has purposes, and prefers one thing to another. And on this view it made the universe, partly for purposes we do not know, but partly, at any rate, in order to produce creatures like itself—I mean, like itself to the extent of having minds. Please do not think that one of these views was held a long time ago and that the other has gradually taken its place. Wherever there have been thinking men both views turn up. And note this too. You cannot find out which view is the right one by science in the ordinary sense. Science works by experiments. It watches how things behave. Every scientific statement in the long run, however complicated it looks, really means something like, "I pointed the telescope to such and such a part of the sky at 2:20 A.M. on January 15th and saw so-and-so," or, "I put some of this stuff in a pot and heated it to such-and-such a temperature and it did so-and-so." Do not think I am saying anything against science: I am only saying what its job is. And the more scientific a man is, the more (I believe) he would agree with me that this is the job of science—and a very useful and necessary job it is too. But why anything comes to be there at all, and whether there is anything behind the things science observes—something of a different kind—this is not a scientific question. If there is "Something Behind," then either it will have to remain altogether unknown to men or else make itself known in some different way. The statement that there is any such thing, and the statement that there

*See Note at the end of this chapter.

is no such thing, are neither of them statements that science can make. And real scientists do not usually make them. It is usually the journalists and popular novelists who have picked up a few odds and ends of half-baked science from textbooks who go in for them. After all, it is really a matter of common sense. Supposing science ever became complete so that it knew every single thing in the whole universe. Is it not plain that the questions, "Why is there a universe?" "Why does it go on as it does?" "Has it any meaning?" would remain just as they were?

Now the position would be quite hopeless but for this. There is one thing, and only one, in the whole universe which we know more about than we could learn from external observation. That one thing is Man. We do not merely observe men, we *are* men. In this case we have, so to speak, inside information; we are in the know. And because of that, we know that men find themselves under a moral law, which they did not make, and cannot quite forget even when they try, and which they know they ought to obey. Notice the following point. Anyone studying Man from the outside as we study electricity or cabbages, not knowing our language and consequently not able to get any inside knowledge from us, but merely observing what we did, would never get the slightest evidence that we had this moral law. How could he? for his observations would only show what we did, and the moral law is about what we ought to do. In the same way, if there were anything above or behind the observed facts in the case of stones or the weather, we, by studying them from outside, could never hope to discover it.

The position of the question, then, is like this. We want to know whether the universe simply happens to be what it is for no reason or whether there is a power behind it that makes it what it is. Since that power, if it exists, would be not one of the observed facts but a reality which makes them, no mere observation of the facts can find it. There is only one case in which we can know whether there is anything more, namely our own case. And in that one case we find there is. Or put it the other way round. If there was a controlling power outside the universe, it could not show itself to us as one of the facts inside the universe—no more than the architect of a house could actually be a wall or staircase or fireplace in that house. The only way in which we could expect it to show itself would be inside ourselves as an influence or a command trying to get us to behave in a certain way. And that is just what we do find inside ourselves. Surely this ought to arouse our suspicions? In the only case where you can expect to get an answer, the answer turns out to be Yes; and in the other cases, where you do not get an answer, you see why you do not. Suppose someone asked me, when I see a man in a blue uniform going down the street leaving little paper packets at each house, why I suppose that they contain letters? I should reply, "Because whenever he leaves a similar little packet for me I find it does contain a letter." And if he then objected, "But you've never seen all these letters which you think the other people are getting," I should say, "Of course not, and I shouldn't expect to, because they're not addressed to me. I'm explaining the packets I'm not allowed to open by the ones I am allowed to open." It is the same about this question. The only packet I am allowed to open is Man. When I do, especially when I open that particular man called Myself, I find that I do not exist on my own, that I am under a law; that somebody or something wants me to behave in a certain way. I do not, of course, think that if I could get inside a stone or a tree I should find exactly the same thing, just as I do not think all the other people in the street get the same letters as I do. I should expect, for instance, to find that the stone had to obey the law of gravity—that whereas the sender of the letters merely tells me to obey the law of my human nature, He compels the stone to obey the laws of its stony nature. But I should expect to find that there was, so to speak, a sender of letters in both cases, a Power behind the facts, a Director, a Guide.

Do not think I am going faster than I really am. I am not yet within a hundred miles of the God of Christian theology. All I have got to is a Something which is directing the universe, and which appears in me as a law urging me to do right and making me feel responsible and uncomfortable when I do wrong. I think we have to assume it is more like a mind than it is like anything else we know—because after all the only other thing we know is matter and you can hardly imagine a bit of matter giving instructions. But, of course, it need not be very like a mind, still less like a person. In the next chapter we shall see if we can find out anything more about it. But one word of warning. There has been a great deal of soft soap talked about God for the last hundred years. That is not what I am offering. You can cut all that out.

NOTE.—In order to keep this section short enough when it was given on the air, I mentioned only the Materialist view and the Religious view. But to be complete I ought to mention the In-between view called Life-Force philosophy, or Creative Evolution, or Emergent Evolution. The wittiest expositions of it come in the works of Bernard Shaw, but the most profound ones in those of Bergson. People who hold this view say that the small variations by which life on this planet "evolved" from the lowest forms to Man were not due to chance but to the "striving" or "purposiveness" of a Life-Force. When people say this we must ask them whether by Life-Force they mean something with a mind or not. If they do, then "a mind bringing life into existence and leading it to perfection" is really a God, and their view is thus identical with the Religious. If they do not, then what is the sense in saying that something without a mind "strives" or has "purposes"? This seems to me fatal to their view. One reason why many people find Creative Evolution so attractive is that it gives one much of the emotional comfort of believing in God and none of the less pleasant consequences. When you are feeling fit and the sun is shining and you do not want to believe that the whole universe is a mere mechanical dance of atoms, it is nice to be able to think of this great mysterious Force rolling on through the centuries and carrying you on its crest. If, on the other hand, you want to do something rather shabby, the Life-Force, being only a blind force, with no morals and no mind, will never interfere with you like that troublesome God we learned about when we were children. The Life-Force is a sort of tame God. You can switch it on when you want, but it will not bother you. All the thrills of religion and none of the cost. Is the Life-Force the greatest achievement of wishful thinking the world has yet seen?

CHAPTER 5
We Have Cause to Be Uneasy

❋

I ENDED MY LAST CHAPTER with the idea that in the Moral Law somebody or something from beyond the material universe was actually getting at us. And I expect when I reached that point some of you felt a certain annoyance. You may even have thought that I had played a trick on you—that I had been carefully wrapping up to look like philosophy what turns out to be one more "religious jaw." You may have felt you were ready to listen to me as long as you thought I had anything new to say; but if it turns out to be only religion, well, the world has tried that and you cannot put the clock back. If anyone is feeling that way I should like to say three things to him.

First, as to putting the clock back. Would you think I was joking if I said that you can put a clock back, and that if the clock is wrong it is often a very sensible thing to do? But I would rather get away from that whole idea of clocks. We all want progress. But progress means getting nearer to the place where you want to be. And if you have taken a wrong turning, then to go forward does not get you any nearer. If you are on the wrong road, progress means doing an about-turn and walking back to the right road; and in that case the man who turns back soonest is the most progressive man. We have all seen this when doing arithmetic. When I have started a sum the wrong way, the sooner I admit this and go back and start over again, the faster I shall get on. There is nothing progressive about being pigheaded and refusing to admit a mistake. And I think if you look at the present state of the world, it is pretty plain that humanity has been making some big mistake. We are on the wrong road. And if that is so, we must go back. Going back is the quickest way on.

Then, secondly, this has not yet turned exactly into a "religious jaw." We have not yet got as far as the God of any actual religion, still less the God of that particular religion called Christianity. We have only got as far as a Somebody or Something behind the Moral Law. We are not taking anything from the Bible or the Churches, we are trying to see what we can find out about this Somebody on our own steam. And I want to make it quite clear that what we find out on our own steam is something that gives us a shock. We have two bits of evidence about the Somebody. One is the universe He has made. If we used that as our only clue, then I think we should have to conclude that He was a great artist (for the universe is a very beautiful place), but also that He is quite merciless and no friend to man (for the universe is a very dangerous and terrifying place). The other bit of evidence is that Moral Law which He has put into our minds. And this is a better bit of evidence than the other, because it is inside information. You find out more about God from the Moral Law than from the universe in general just as you find out more about a man by listening to his conversation than by looking at a house he has built. Now, from this second bit of evidence we conclude that the Being behind the universe is intensely interested in right conduct—in fair play, unselfishness, courage, good faith, honesty and truthfulness. In that sense we should agree with the account given by Christianity and some other religions, that God is "good." But do not let us go too fast here. The Moral Law does not give us any grounds for thinking that God is "good" in the sense of being indulgent, or soft, or sympathetic. There is nothing indulgent about the Moral Law. It is as hard as nails. It tells you to do the straight thing and it does not seem to care how painful, or dangerous, or difficult it is to do. If God is like the Moral Law, then He is not soft. It is no use, at this stage, saying that what you mean by a "good" God is a God who can forgive. You are going too quickly. Only a Person can forgive. And we have not yet got as far as a personal God—only as far as a power, behind the Moral Law, and more like a mind than it is like anything else. But it may still be very unlike a Person. If it is pure impersonal mind, there may be no sense in asking it to make allowances for you or let you off, just as there is no sense in asking the multiplication table to let you off when you do your sums wrong. You are bound to get the wrong answer. And it is no use either saying that if there is a God of that sort—an impersonal absolute goodness—then you do not like Him and are not going to bother about Him. For the trouble is that one part of you is on His side and really agrees with His disapproval of human greed and trickery and exploitation. You may want Him to make an exception in your own case, to let you off this one time; but you know at bottom that unless the power behind the world really and unalterably detests that sort of behaviour, then He cannot be good. On the other hand, we know that if there does exist an absolute goodness it must hate most of what we do. That is the terrible fix we are in. If the universe is not governed by an absolute goodness, then all our efforts are in the long run hopeless. But if it is, then we are making ourselves enemies to that goodness every day, and are not in the least likely to do any better tomorrow, and so our case is hopeless again. We cannot do without it, and we cannot do with it. God is the only comfort, He is also the supreme terror: the thing we most need and the thing we most want to hide from. He is our only possible ally, and we have made ourselves His enemies. Some people talk as if meeting the gaze of absolute goodness would be fun. They need to think again. They are still only playing with religion. Goodness is either the great safety or the great danger—according to the way you react to it. And we have reacted the wrong way.

Now my third point. When I chose to get to my real subject in this roundabout way, I was not trying to play any kind of trick on you. I had a different reason. My reason was that Christianity simply does not make sense until you have faced the sort of facts I have been describing. Christianity tells people to repent and promises them forgiveness. It therefore has nothing (as far as I know) to say to people who do not know they have done anything to repent of and who do not feel that they need any forgiveness. It is after you have realised that there is a real Moral Law, and a Power behind the law, and that you have broken that law and put yourself wrong with that Power—it is after all this, and not a moment sooner, that Christianity begins to talk. When you know you are sick, you will listen to the doctor. When you have realised that our position is nearly desperate you will begin to understand what the Christians are talking about. They offer an explanation of how we got into our present state of both hating goodness and loving it. They offer an explanation of how God can be this impersonal mind at the back of the Moral Law and yet also a Person. They tell you how the demands of this law, which you and I cannot meet, have been met on our behalf, how God Himself becomes a man to save man from the disapproval of God. It is an old story and if you want to go into it you will no doubt consult people who have more authority to talk about it than I have. All I am doing is to ask people to face the facts—to understand the questions which Christianity claims to answer. And they are very terrifying facts. I wish it was possible to say something more agreeable. But I must say what I think true. Of course, I quite agree that the Christian religion is, in the long run, a thing of unspeakable comfort. But it does not begin in comfort; it begins in the dismay I have been describing, and it is no use at all trying to go on to that comfort without first going through that dismay. In religion, as in war and everything else, comfort is the one thing you cannot get by looking for it. If you look for truth, you may find comfort in the end: if you look for comfort you will not get either comfort or truth—only soft soap and wishful thinking to begin with and, in the end, despair. Most of us have got over the pre-war wishful thinking about international politics. It is time we did the same about religion.

BOOK II

What Christians Believe

The Rival Conceptions of God

I HAVE BEEN ASKED to tell you what Christians believe, and I am going to begin by telling you one thing that Christians do not need to believe. If you are a Christian you do not have to believe that all the other religions are simply wrong all through. If you are an atheist you do have to believe that the main point in all the religions of the whole world is simply one huge mistake. If you are a Christian, you are free to think that all these religions, even the queerest ones, contain at least some hint of the truth. When I was an atheist I had to try to persuade myself that most of the human race have always been wrong about the question that mattered to them most; when I became a Christian I was able to take a more liberal view. But, of course, being a Christian does mean thinking that where Christianity differs from other religions, Christianity is right and they are wrong. As in arithmetic—there is only one right answer to a sum, and all other answers are wrong: but some of the wrong answers are much nearer being right than others.

The first big division of humanity is into the majority, who believe in some kind of God or gods, and the minority who do not. On this point, Christianity lines up with the majority—lines up with ancient Greeks and Romans, modern savages, Stoics, Platonists, Hindus, Mohammedans, etc., against the modern Western European materialist.

Now I go on to the next big division. People who all believe in God can be divided according to the sort of God they believe in. There are two very different ideas on this subject. One of them is the idea that He is beyond good and evil. We humans call one thing good and another thing bad. But according to scme people that is merely our human point of view. These people would say that the wiser you become the less you would want to call anything good or bad, and the more clearly you would see that everything is good in one way and bad in another, and that nothing could have been different. Consequently, these people think that long before you got anywhere near the divine point of view the distinction would have disappeared altogether. We call a cancer bad, they would say, because it kills a man; but you might just as well call a successful surgeon bad because he kills a cancer. It all depends on the point of view. The other and opposite idea is that God is quite definitely "good" or "righteous," a God who takes sides, who loves love and hates hatred, who wants us to behave in one way and not in another. The first of these views—the one that thinks God beyond good and evil—is called Pantheism. It was held by the great Prussian philosopher Hegel and, as far as I can understand them, by the Hindus. The other view is held by Jews, Mohammedans and Christians.

And with this big difference between Pantheism and the Christian idea of God, there usually goes another. Pantheists usually believe that God, so to speak, animates the universe as you animate your body: that the universe almost *is* God, so that if it did not exist He would not exist either, and anything you find in the universe is a part of God. The Christian idea is quite different. They think God invented and made the universe—like a man making a picture or composing a tune. A painter is not a picture, and he does not die if his picture is destroyed. You may say, "He's put a lot of himself into it," but you only mean that all its beauty and interest has come out of his head. His skill is not in the picture in the same way that it is in his head, or even in his hands. I expect you see how this difference between Pantheists and Christians hangs together with the other one. If you do not take the distinction between good and bad very seriously, then it is easy to say that anything you find in this world is a part of God. But, of course, if you think some things really bad, and God really good, then you cannot talk like that. You must believe that God is separate from the world and that some of the things we see in it are contrary to His will. Confronted with a cancer or a slum the Pantheist can say, "If you could only see it from the divine point of view, you would realise that this also is God." The Christian replies, "Don't talk damned nonsense."* For Christianity is a fighting religion. It thinks God made the world—that space and time, heat and cold, and all the colours and tastes, and all the animals and vegetables, are things that God "made up out of His head" as a man makes up a story. But it also thinks that a great many things have gone wrong with the world that God made and that God insists, and insists very loudly, on our putting them right again.

And, of course, that raises a very big question. If a good God made the world why has it gone wrong? And for many years I simply refused to listen to the Christian answers to this question, because I kept on feeling "Whatever you say, and however clever your arguments are, isn't it much simpler and easier to say that the world was not made by any intelligent power? Aren't all your arguments simply a complicated attempt to avoid the obvious?" But then that threw me back into another difficulty.

My argument against God was that the universe seemed so cruel and unjust. But how had I got this idea of *just* and *unjust*? A man does not call a line crooked unless he has some idea of a straight line. What was I comparing this universe with when

---

*One listener complained of the word *damned* as frivolous swearing. But I mean exactly what I say—nonsense that is *damned* is under God's curse, and will (apart from God's grace) lead those who believe it to eternal death.

I called it unjust? If the whole show was bad and senseless from A to Z, so to speak, why did I, who was supposed to be part of the show, find myself in such violent reaction against it? A man feels wet when he falls into water, because man is not a water animal: a fish would not feel wet. Of course I could have given up my idea of justice by saying it was nothing but a private idea of my own. But if I did that, then my argument against God collapsed too—for the argument depended on saying that the world was really unjust, not simply that it did not happen to please my private fancies. Thus in the very act of trying to prove that God did not exist—in other words, that the whole of reality was senseless—I found I was forced to assume that one part of reality—namely my idea of justice—was full of sense. Consequently atheism turns out to be too simple. If the whole universe has no meaning, we should never have found out that it has no meaning: just as, if there were no light in the universe and therefore no creatures with eyes, we should never know it was dark. *Dark* would be without meaning.

CHAPTER 2

The Invasion

❉

Very well then, atheism is too simple. And I will tell you another view that is also too simple. It is the view I call Christianity-and-water, the view which simply says there is a good God in Heaven and everything is all right—leaving out all the difficult and terrible doctrines about sin and hell and the devil, and the redemption. Both these are boys' philosophies.

It is no good asking for a simple religion. After all, real things are not simple. They look simple, but they are not. The table I am sitting at looks simple: but ask a scientist to tell you what it is really made of—all about the atoms and how the light waves rebound from them and hit my eye and what they do to the optic nerve and what it does to my brain—and, of course, you find that what we call "seeing a table" lands you in mysteries and complications which you can hardly get to the end of. A child saying a child's prayer looks simple. And if you are content to stop there, well and good. But if you are not—and the modern world usually is not—if you want to go on and ask what is really happening—then you must be prepared for something difficult. If we ask for something more than simplicity, it is silly then to complain that the something more is not simple.

Very often, however, this silly procedure is adopted by people who are not silly, but who, consciously or unconsciously, want to destroy Christianity. Such people put up a version of Christianity suitable for a child of six and make that the object of their attack. When you try to explain the Christian doctrine as it is really held by an instructed adult, they then complain that you are making their heads turn round and that it is all too complicated and that if there really were a God they are sure He would have made "religion" simple, because simplicity is so beautiful, etc. You must be on your guard against these people for they will change their ground every minute and only waste your time. Notice, too, their idea of God "making religion simple": as if "religion" were something God invented, and not His statement to us of certain quite unalterable facts about His own nature.

Besides being complicated, reality, in my experience, is usually odd. It is not neat, not obvious, not what you expect. For instance, when you have grasped that the earth and the other planets all go round the sun, you would naturally expect that all the planets were made to match—all at equal distances from each other, say, or distances that regularly increased, or all the same size, or else getting bigger or smaller as you go farther from the sun. In fact, you find no rhyme or reason (that we can see) about either the sizes or the distances; and some of them have one moon, one has four, one has two, some have none, and one has a ring.

Reality, in fact, is usually something you could not have guessed. That is one of the reasons I believe Christianity. It is a religion you could not have guessed. If it offered us just the kind of universe we had always expected, I should feel we were making it up. But, in fact, it is not the sort of thing anyone would have made up. It has just that queer twist about it that real things have. So let us leave behind all these boys' philosophies—these over-simple answers. The problem is not simple and the answer is not going to be simple either.

What is the problem? A universe that contains much that is obviously bad and apparently meaningless, but containing creatures like ourselves who know that it is bad and meaning-less. There are only two views that face all the facts. One is the Christian view that this is a good world that has gone wrong, but still retains the memory of what it ought to have been. The other is the view called Dualism. Dualism means the belief that there are two equal and independent powers at the back of everything, one of them good and the other bad, and that this universe is the battlefield in which they fight out an endless war. I personally think that next to Christianity Dualism is the manliest and most sensible creed on the market. But it has a catch in it.

The two powers, or spirits, or gods—the good one and the bad one—are supposed to be quite independent. They both existed from all eternity. Neither of them made the other, nei-ther of them has any more right than the other to call itself God. Each presumably thinks it is good and thinks the other bad. One of them likes hatred and cruelty, the other likes love and mercy, and each backs its own view. Now what do we mean when we call one of them the Good Power and the other the Bad Power? Either we are merely saying that we happen to prefer the one to the other—like preferring beer to cider—or else we are saying that, whatever the two powers think about it, and whichever we humans, at the moment, happen to like, one of them is actually wrong, actually mistaken, in regarding itself as good. Now if we mean merely that we hap-pen to prefer the first, then we must give up talking about good and evil at all. For good means what you ought to prefer quite regardless of what you happen to like at any given mo-ment. If "being good" meant simply joining the side you hap-pened to fancy, for no real reason, then good would not deserve to be called good. So we must mean that one of the two powers is actually wrong and the other actually right.

But the moment you say that, you are putting into the uni-verse a third thing in addition to the two Powers: some law or standard or rule of good which one of the powers conforms to and the other fails to conform to. But since the two powers are judged by this standard, then this standard, or the Being who made this standard, is farther back and higher up than either of them, and He will be the real God. In fact, what we meant by calling them good and bad turns out to be that one of them is in a right relation to the real ultimate God and the other in a wrong relation to Him.

The same point can be made in a different way. If Dualism is true, then the bad Power must be a being who likes badness for its own sake. But in reality we have no experience of anyone liking badness just because it is bad. The nearest we can get to it is in cruelty. But in real life people are cruel for one of two reasons—either because they are sadists, that is, because they have a sexual perversion which makes cruelty a cause of sensual pleasure to them, or else for the sake of something they are going to get out of it—money, or power, or safety. But pleasure, money, power, and safety are all, as far as they go, good things. The badness consists in pursuing them by the wrong method, or in the wrong way, or too much. I do not mean, of course, that the people who do this are not desperately wicked. I do mean that wickedness, when you examine it, turns out to be the pursuit of some good in the wrong way. You can be good for the mere sake of goodness: you cannot be bad for the mere sake of badness. You can do a kind action when you are not feeling kind and when it gives you no pleasure, simply because kindness is right; but no one ever did a cruel action simply because cruelty is wrong—only because cruelty was pleasant or useful to him. In other words badness cannot succeed even in being bad in the same way in which goodness is good. Goodness is, so to speak, itself: badness is only spoiled goodness. And there must be something good first before it can be spoiled. We called sadism a sexual perversion; but you must first have the idea of a normal sexuality before you can talk of its being perverted; and you can see which is the perversion, because you can explain the perverted from the normal, and cannot explain the normal from the perverted. It follows that this Bad

Power, who is supposed to be on an equal footing with the Good Power, and to love badness in the same way as the Good Power loves goodness, is a mere bogy. In order to be bad he must have good things to want and then to pursue in the wrong way: he must have impulses which were originally good in order to be able to pervert them. But if he is bad he cannot supply himself either with good things to desire or with good impulses to pervert. He must be getting both from the Good Power. And if so, then he is not independent. He is part of the Good Power's world: he was made either by the Good Power or by some power above them both.

Put it more simply still. To be bad, he must exist and have intelligence and will. But existence, intelligence and will are in themselves good. Therefore he must be getting them from the Good Power: even to be bad he must borrow or steal from his opponent. And do you now begin to see why Christianity has always said that the devil is a fallen angel? That is not a mere story for the children. It is a real recognition of the fact that evil is a parasite, not an original thing. The powers which enable evil to carry on are powers given it by goodness. All the things which enable a bad man to be effectively bad are in themselves good things—resolution, cleverness, good looks, existence itself. That is why Dualism, in a strict sense, will not work.

But I freely admit that real Christianity (as distinct from Christianity-and-water) goes much nearer to Dualism than people think. One of the things that surprised me when I first read the New Testament seriously was that it talked so much about a Dark Power in the universe—a mighty evil spirit who was held to be the Power behind death and disease, and sin. The difference is that Christianity thinks this Dark Power was created by God, and was good when he was created, and went wrong. Christianity agrees with Dualism that this universe is at war. But it does not think this is a war between independent powers. It thinks it is a civil war, a rebellion, and that we are living in a part of the universe occupied by the rebel.

Enemy-occupied territory—that is what this world is. Christianity is the story of how the rightful king has landed, you might say landed in disguise, and is calling us all to take part in a great campaign of sabotage. When you go to church you are really listening-in to the secret wireless from our friends: that is why the enemy is so anxious to prevent us from going. He does it by playing on our conceit and laziness and intellectual snobbery. I know someone will ask me, "Do you really mean, at this time of day, to re-introduce our old friend the devil—hoofs and horns and all?" Well, what the time of day has to do with it I do not know. And I am not particular about the hoofs and horns. But in other respects my answer is "Yes, I do." I do not claim to know anything about his personal appearance. If anybody really wants to know him better I would say to that person, "Don't worry. If you really want to, you will. Whether you'll like it when you do is another question."

CHAPTER 3
The Shocking Alternative

❋

CHRISTIANS, THEN, BELIEVE that an evil power has made himself for the present the Prince of this World. And, of course, that raises problems. Is this state of affairs in accordance with God's will or not? If it is, He is a strange God, you will say: and if it is not, how can anything happen contrary to the will of a being with absolute power?

But anyone who has been in authority knows how a thing can be in accordance with your will in one way and not in another. It may be quite sensible for a mother to say to the children, "I'm not going to go and make you tidy the schoolroom every night. You've got to learn to keep it tidy on your own." Then she goes up one night and finds the Teddy bear and the ink and the French Grammar all lying in the grate. That is against her will. She would prefer the children to be tidy. But on the other hand, it is her will which has left the children free to be untidy. The same thing arises in any regiment, or trade union, or school. You make a thing voluntary and then half the people do not do it. That is not what you willed, but your will has made it possible.

It is probably the same in the universe. God created things which had free will. That means creatures which can go either wrong or right. Some people think they can imagine a creature which was free but had no possibility of going wrong; I cannot. If a thing is free to be good it is also free to be bad. And free will is what has made evil possible. Why, then, did God give them free will? Because free will, though it makes evil possible, is also the only thing that makes possible any love or goodness or joy worth having. A world of automata—of creatures that worked like machines—would hardly be worth creating. The happiness which God designs for His higher creatures is the happiness of being freely, voluntarily united to Him and to each other in an ecstasy of love and delight compared with which the most rapturous love between a man and a woman on this earth is mere milk and water. And for that they must be free.

Of course God knew what would happen if they used their freedom the wrong way: apparently He thought it worth the risk. Perhaps we feel inclined to disagree with Him. But there is a difficulty about disagreeing with God. He is the source from which all your reasoning power comes: you could not be right and He wrong any more than a stream can rise higher than its own source. When you are arguing against Him you are arguing against the very power that makes you able to argue at all: it is like cutting off the branch you are sitting on. If God thinks this state of war in the universe a price worth paying for free will—that is, for making a live world in which creatures can do real good or harm and something of real importance can happen, instead of a toy world which only moves when He pulls the strings—then we may take it it is worth paying.

When we have understood about free will, we shall see how silly it is to ask, as somebody once asked me: "Why did God make a creature of such rotten stuff that it went wrong?" The better stuff a creature is made of—the cleverer and stronger and freer it is—then the better it will be if it goes right, but also the worse it will be if it goes wrong. A cow cannot be very good or very bad; a dog can be both better or worse; a child better and worse still; an ordinary man, still more so; a man of genius, still more so; a superhuman spirit best—or worst—of all.

How did the Dark Power go wrong? Here, no doubt, we ask a question to which human beings cannot give an answer with any certainty. A reasonable (and traditional) guess, based on our own experiences of going wrong, can, however, be offered. The moment you have a self at all, there is a possibility of putting yourself first—wanting to be the centre—wanting to be God, in fact. That was the sin of Satan: and that was the sin he taught the human race. Some people think the fall of man had something to do with sex, but that is a mistake. (The story in the Book of Genesis rather suggests that some corruption in our sexual nature followed the fall and was its result, not its cause.) What Satan put into the heads of our remote ancestors was the idea that they could "be like gods"—could set up on their own as if they had created themselves—be their own masters—invent some sort of happiness for themselves outside God, apart from God. And out of that hopeless attempt has come nearly all that we call human history— money, poverty, ambition, war, prostitution, classes, empires, slavery—the long terrible story of man trying to find something other than God which will make him happy.

The reason why it can never succeed is this. God made us: invented us as a man invents an engine. A car is made to run on gasoline, and it would not run properly on anything else. Now God designed the human machine to run on Himself. He Himself is the fuel our spirits were designed to burn, or the food our spirits were designed to feed on. There is no other. That is why it is just no good asking God to make us happy in our own way without bothering about religion. God cannot give us a happiness and peace apart from Himself, because it is not there. There is no such thing.

That is the key to history. Terrific energy is expended—civilisations are built up—excellent institutions devised; but each time something goes wrong. Some fatal flaw always brings the selfish and cruel people to the top and it all slides back into misery and ruin. In fact, the machine conks. It seems to start up all right and runs a few yards, and then it breaks down. They are trying to run it on the wrong juice. That is what Satan has done to us humans.

And what did God do? First of all He left us conscience, the sense of right and wrong: and all through history there have been people trying (some of them very hard) to obey it. None of them ever quite succeeded. Secondly, He sent the human race what I call good dreams: I mean those queer stories scattered all through the heathen religions about a god who dies and comes to life again and, by his death, has somehow given new life to men. Thirdly, He selected one particular people and spent several centuries hammering into their heads the sort of God He was—that there was only one of Him and that He cared about right conduct. Those people were the Jews, and the Old Testament gives an account of the hammering process.

Then comes the real shock. Among these Jews there suddenly turns up a man who goes about talking as if He was God. He claims to forgive sins. He says He has always existed. He says He is coming to judge the world at the end of time. Now let us get this clear. Among Pantheists, like the Indians, anyone might say that he was a part of God, or one with God: there would be nothing very odd about it. But this man, since He was a Jew, could not mean that kind of God. God in their language, meant the Being outside the world Who had made it and was infinitely different from anything else. And when you have grasped that, you will see that what this man said was, quite simply, the most shocking thing that has ever been uttered by human lips.

One part of the claim tends to slip past us unnoticed because we have heard it so often that we no longer see what it amounts to. I mean the claim to forgive sins: any sins. Now unless the speaker is God, this is really so preposterous as to be comic. We can all understand how a man forgives offences against himself. You tread on my toe and I forgive you, you steal my money and I forgive you. But what should we make of a man, himself unrobbed and untrodden on, who announced that he forgave you for treading on other men's toes and stealing other men's money? Asinine fatuity is the kindest description we should give of his conduct. Yet this is what Jesus did. He told people that their sins were forgiven, and never waited to consult all the other people whom their sins had undoubtedly injured. He unhesitatingly behaved as if He was the party chiefly concerned, the person chiefly offended in all offences. This makes sense only if He really was the God whose laws are broken and whose love is wounded in every sin. In the mouth of any speaker who is not God, these words would imply what I can only regard as a silliness and conceit unrivaled by any other character in history.

Yet (and this is the strange, significant thing) even His enemies, when they read the Gospels, do not usually get the impression of silliness and conceit. Still less do unprejudiced readers. Christ says that He is "humble and meek" and we believe Him; not noticing that, if He were merely a man, humility and meekness are the very last characteristics we could attribute to some of His sayings.

I am trying here to prevent anyone saying the really foolish thing that people often say about Him: "I'm ready to accept Jesus as a great moral teacher, but I don't accept His claim to be God." That is the one thing we must not say. A man who was merely a man and said the sort of things Jesus said would not be a great moral teacher. He would either be a lunatic—on a level with the man who says he is a poached egg—or else he would be the Devil of Hell. You must make your choice. Either this man was, and is, the Son of God: or else a madman or something worse. You can shut Him up for a fool, you can spit at Him and kill Him as a demon; or you can fall at His feet and call Him Lord and God. But let us not come with any patronising nonsense about His being a great human teacher. He has not left that open to us. He did not intend to.

CHAPTER 4

The Perfect Penitent

❋

WE ARE FACED, then, with a frightening alternative. This man we are talking about either was (and is) just what He said or else a lunatic, or something worse. Now it seems to me obvious that He was neither a lunatic nor a fiend: and consequently, however strange or terrifying or unlikely it may seem, I have to accept the view that He was and is God. God has landed on this enemy-occupied world in human form.

And now, what was the purpose of it all? What did He come to do? Well, to teach, of course; but as soon as you look into the New Testament or any other Christian writing you will find they are constantly talking about something different— about His death and His coming to life again. It is obvious that Christians think the chief point of the story lies here. They think the main thing He came to earth to do was to suffer and be killed.

Now before I became a Christian I was under the impression that the first thing Christians had to believe was one particular theory as to what the point of this dying was. According to that theory God wanted to punish men for having deserted and joined the Great Rebel, but Christ volunteered to be punished instead, and so God let us off. Now I admit that even this theory does not seem to me quite so immoral and so silly as it used to; but that is not the point I want to make. What I came to see later on was that neither this theory nor any other is Christianity. The central Christian belief is that Christ's death has somehow put us right with God and given us a fresh start. Theories as to how it did this are another matter. A good many different theories have been held as to how it works; what all Christians are agreed on is that it does work. I will tell you what I think it is like. All sensible people know that if you are tired and hungry a meal will do you good. But the modern theory of nourishment—all about the vitamins and proteins—is a different thing. People ate their dinners and felt better long before the theory of vitamins was every heard of: and if the theory of vitamins is some day abandoned they will go on eating their dinners just the same. Theories about Christ's death are not Christianity: they are explanations about how it works. Christians would not all agree as to how important these theories are. My own church—the Church of England—does not lay down any one of them as the right one. The Church of Rome goes a bit further. But I think they will all agree that the thing itself is infinitely more important than any explanations that theologians have produced. I think they would probably admit that no explanation will ever be quite adequate to the reality. But as I said in the preface to this book, I am only a layman, and at this point we are getting into deep water. I can only tell you, for what it is worth, how I, personally, look at the matter.

On my view the theories are not themselves the thing you are asked to accept. Many of you no doubt have read Jeans or Eddington. What they do when they want to explain the atom, or something of that sort, is to give you a description out of which you can make a mental picture. But then they warn you that this picture is not what the scientists actually believe. What the scientists believe is a mathematical formula. The pictures are there only to help you to understand the formula. They are not really true in the way the formula is; they do not give you the real thing but only something more or less like it.

They are only meant to help, and if they do not help you can drop them. The thing itself cannot be pictured, it can only be expressed mathematically. We are in the same boat here. We believe that the death of Christ is just that point in history at which something absolutely unimaginable from outside shows through into our own world. And if we cannot picture even the atoms of which our own world is built, of course we are not going to be able to picture this. Indeed, if we found that we could fully understand it, that very fact would show it was not what it professes to be—the inconceivable, the uncreated, the thing from beyond nature, striking down into nature like lightning. You may ask what good it will be to us if we do not understand it. But that is easily answered. A man can eat his dinner without understanding exactly how food nourishes him. A man can accept what Christ has done without knowing how it works: indeed, he certainly would not know how it works until he has accepted it.

We are told that Christ was killed for us, that His death has washed out our sins, and that by dying He disabled death itself. That is the formula. That is Christianity. That is what has to be believed. Any theories we build up as to how Christ's death did all this are, in my view, quite secondary: mere plans or diagrams to be left alone if they do not help us, and, even if they do help us, not to be confused with the thing itself. All the same, some of these theories are worth looking at.

The one most people have heard is the one I mentioned before—the one about being let off because Christ had volunteered to bear a punishment instead of us. Now on the face of it that is a very silly theory. If God was prepared to let us off, why on earth did He not do so? And what possible point could there be in punishing an innocent person instead? None at all that I can see, if you are thinking of punishment in the police-court sense. On the other hand, if you think of a debt, there is plenty of point in a person who has some assets paying it on behalf of someone who has not. Or if you take "paying the penalty," not in the sense of being punished, but in the more general sense of "standing the racket" or "footing the bill," then, of course, it is a matter of common experience that, when one person has got himself into a hole, the trouble of getting him out usually falls on a kind friend.

Now what was the sort of "hole" man had got himself into? He had tried to set up on his own, to behave as if he belonged to himself. In other words, fallen man is not simply an imperfect creature who needs improvement: he is a rebel who must lay down his arms. Laying down your arms, surrendering, saying you are sorry, realising that you have been on the wrong track and getting ready to start life over again from the ground floor—that is the only way out of a "hole." This process of surrender—this movement full speed astern—is what Christians call repentance. Now repentance is no fun at all. It is something much harder than merely eating humble pie. It means unlearning all the self-conceit and self-will that we have been training ourselves into for thousands of years. It means killing part of yourself, undergoing a kind of death. In fact, it needs a good man to repent. And here comes the catch. Only a bad person needs to repent: only a good person can repent perfectly. The worse you are the more you need it and the less you can do it. The only person who could do it perfectly would be a perfect person—and he would not need it.

Remember, this repentance, this willing submission to humiliation and a kind of death, is not something God demands of you before He will take you back and which He could let you off if He chose: it is simply a description of what going back to Him is like. If you ask God to take you back without it, you are really asking Him to let you go back without going back. It cannot happen. Very well, then, we must go through with it. But the same badness which makes us need it, makes us unable to do it. Can we do it if God helps us? Yes, but what do we mean when we talk of God helping us? We mean God putting into us a bit of Himself, so to speak. He lends us a little of His reasoning powers and that is how we think: He puts a little of His love into us and that is how we love one another. When you teach a child writing, you hold its hand while it forms the letters: that is, it forms the letter because you are forming them. We love and reason because God loves and reasons and holds our hand while we do it. Now if we had not fallen, that would be all plain sailing. But unfortunately we now need God's help in order to do something which God, in His own nature, never does at all—to surrender, to suffer, to submit, to die. Nothing in God's nature corresponds to this process at all. So that the one road for which we now need God's leadership most of all is a road God, in His own nature, has never walked. God can share only what He has: this thing, in His own nature, He has not.

But supposing God became a man—suppose our human nature which can suffer and die was amalgamated with God's nature in one person—then that person could help us. He could surrender His will, and suffer and die, because He was man; and He could do it perfectly because He was God. You and I can go through this process only if God does it in us; but God can do it only if He becomes man. Our attempts at this dying will succeed only if we men share in God's dying, just as our thinking can succeed only because it is a drop out of the ocean of His intelligence: but we cannot share God's dying unless God dies; and He cannot die except by being a man. That is the sense in which He pays our debt, and suffers for us what He Himself need not suffer at all.

I have heard some people complain that if Jesus was God as well as man, then His sufferings and death lose all value in their eyes, "because it must have been so easy for him." Others may (very rightly) rebuke the ingratitude and ungraciousness of this objection; what staggers me is the misunderstanding it betrays. In one sense, of course, those who make it are right. They have even understated their own case. The perfect submission, the perfect suffering, the perfect death were not only easier to Jesus because He was God, but were possible only because He was God. But surely that is a very odd reason for not accepting them? The teacher is able to form the letters for the child because the teacher is grown-up and knows how to write. That, of course, makes it easier for the teacher; and only because it is easier for him can he help the child. If it rejected him because "it's easy for grown-ups" and waited to learn writing from another child who could not write itself (and so had no "unfair" advantage), it would not get on very quickly. If I am drowning in a rapid river, a man who still has one foot on the bank may give me a hand which saves my life. Ought I to shout back (between my gasps) "No, it's not fair! You have an advantage! You're keeping one foot on the bank"? That advantage—call it "unfair" if you like—is the only reason why he can be of any use to me. To what will you look for help if you will not look to that which is stronger than yourself?

Such is my own way of looking at what Christians call the Atonement. But remember this is only one more picture. Do not mistake it for the thing itself: and if it does not help you, drop it.

CHAPTER 5

The Practical Conclusion

❋

THE PERFECT SURRENDER and humiliation were undergone by
Christ: perfect because He was God, surrender and humiliation because He was man. Now the Christian belief is that if
we somehow share the humility and suffering of Christ we
shall also share in His conquest of death and find a new life
after we have died and in it become perfect, and perfectly
happy, creatures. This means something much more than our
trying to follow His teaching. People often ask when the next
step in evolution—the step to something beyond man—will
happen. But on the Christian view, it has happened already.
In Christ a new kind of man appeared: and the new kind of
life which began in Him is to be put into us.

How is this to be done? Now, please remember how we
acquired the old, ordinary kind of life. We derived it from others, from our father and mother and all our ancestors, without
our consent—and by a very curious process, involving pleasure, pain, and danger. A process you would never have
guessed. Most of us spend a good many years in childhood
trying to guess it: and some children, when they are first told,
do not believe it—and I am not sure that I blame them, for it
is very odd. Now the God who arranged that process is the
same God who arranges how the new kind of life—the Christ

life—is to be spread. We must be prepared for it being odd too. He did not consult us when He invented sex: He has not consulted us either when He invented this.

There are three things that spread the Christ life to us: baptism, belief, and that mysterious action which different Christians call by different names—Holy Communion, the Mass, the Lord's Supper. At least, those are the three ordinary methods. I am not saying there may not be special cases where it is spread without one or more of these. I have not time to go into special cases, and I do not know enough. If you are trying in a few minutes to tell a man how to get to Edinburgh you will tell him the trains: he can, it is true, get there by boat or by a plane, but you will hardly bring that in. And I am not saying anything about which of these three things is the most essential. My Methodist friend would like me to say more about belief and less (in proportion) about the other two. But I am not going into that. Anyone who professes to teach you Christian doctrine will, in fact, tell you to use all three, and that is enough for our present purpose.

I cannot myself see why these things should be the conductors of the new kind of life. But then, if one did not happen to know, I should never have seen any connection between a particular physical pleasure and the appearance of a new human being in the world. We have to take reality as it comes to us: there is no good jabbering about what it ought to be like or what we should have expected it to be like. But though I cannot see why it should be so, I can tell you why I believe it is so. I have explained why I have to believe that Jesus was (and is) God. And it seems plain as a matter of history that He taught His followers that the new life was communicated in this way. In other words, I believe it on His authority. Do not be scared by the word authority. Believing things on authority only means believing them because you have been told them by someone you think trustworthy. Ninety-nine per cent of the things you believe are believed on authority. I believe there is such a place as New York. I have not seen it myself. I could not prove by abstract reasoning that there must be such a place. I believe it because reliable people have told me so. The ordinary man believes in the Solar System, atoms, evolution, and the circulation of the blood on authority—because the scientists say so. Every historical statement in the world is believed on authority. None of us has seen the Norman Conquest or the defeat of the Armada. None of us could prove them by pure logic as you prove a thing in mathematics. We believe them simply because people who did see them have left writings that tell us about them: in fact, on authority. A man who jibbed at authority in other things as some people do in religion would have to be content to know nothing all his life.

Do not think I am setting up baptism and belief and the Holy Communion as things that will do instead of your own attempts to copy Christ. Your natural life is derived from your parents; that does not mean it will stay there if you do nothing about it. You can lose it by neglect, or you can drive it away by committing suicide. You have to feed it and look after it. but always remember you are not making it, you are only keeping up a life you got from someone else. In the same way a Christian can lose the Christ-life which has been put into him, and he has to make efforts to keep it. But even the best Christian that ever lived is not acting on his own steam—he is only nourishing or protecting a life he could never have acquired by his own efforts. And that has practical consequences. As long as the natural life is in your body, it will do a lot towards repairing that body. Cut it, and up to a point it will heal, as a dead body would not. A live body is not one that never gets hurt, but one that can to some extent repair itself. In the same way a Christian is not a man who never goes wrong, but a man who is enabled to repent and pick himself up and begin over again after each stumble—because the Christ-life is inside him, repairing him all the time, enabling him to repeat (in some degree) the kind of voluntary death which Christ Himself carried out.

That is why the Christian is in a different position from other people who are trying to be good. They hope, by being good, to please God if there is one; or—if they think there is not—at least they hope to deserve approval from good men. But the Christian thinks any good he does comes from the Christ-life inside him. He does not think God will love us because we are good, but that God will make us good because He loves us; just as the roof of a greenhouse does not attract the sun because it is bright, but becomes bright because the sun shines on it.

And let me make it quite clear that when Christians say the Christ-life is in them, they do not mean simply something mental or moral. When they speak of being "in Christ" or of Christ being "in them," this is not simply a way of saying that they are thinking about Christ or copying Him. They mean that Christ is actually operating through them; that the whole mass of Christians are the physical organism through which Christ acts—that we are His fingers and muscles, the cells of His body. And perhaps that explains one or two things. It explains why this new life is spread not only by purely mental acts like belief, but by bodily acts like baptism and Holy Communion. It is not merely the spreading of an idea; it is more like evolution—a biological or super-biological fact. There is no good trying to be more spiritual than God. God never meant man to be a purely spiritual creature. That is why He uses material things like bread and wine to put the new life into us. We may think this rather crude and unspiritual. God does not: He invented eating. He likes matter. He invented it.

Here is another thing that used to puzzle me. Is it not frightfully unfair that this new life should be confined to people who have heard of Christ and been able to believe in Him? But the truth is God has not told us what His arrangements about the other people are. We do know that no man can be saved except through Christ; we do not know that only those who know Him can be saved through Him. But in the meantime, if you are worried about the people outside, the most unreasonable thing you can do is to remain outside yourself. Christians are Christ's body, the organism through which He works. Every addition to that body enables Him to do more. If you want to help those outside you must add your own little cell to the body of Christ who alone can help them. Cutting off a man's fingers would be an odd way of getting him to do more work.

Another possible objection is this. Why is God landing in this enemy-occupied world in disguise and starting a sort of secret society to undermine the devil? Why is He not landing in force, invading it? Is it that He is not strong enough? Well, Christians think He is going to land in force; we do not know when. But we can guess why He is delaying. He wants to give us the chance of joining His side freely. I do not suppose you and I would have thought much of a Frenchman who waited till the Allies were marching into Germany and then announced he was on our side. God will invade. But I wonder whether people who ask God to interfere openly and directly in our world quite realise what it will be like when He does. When that happens, it is the end of the world. When the author walks on to the stage the play is over. God is going to invade, all right: but what is the good of saying you are on His side then, when you see the whole natural universe melting away like a dream and something else—something it never entered your head to conceive—comes crashing in; something so beautiful to some of us and so terrible to others that none of us will have any choice left? For this time it will be God without disguise; something so overwhelming that it will strike either irresistible love or irresistible horror into every creature. It will be too late then to choose your side. There is no use saying you choose to lie down when it has become impossible to stand up. That will not be the time for choosing: it will be the time when we discover which side we really have chosen, whether we realised it before or not. Now, today, this moment, is our chance to choose the right side. God is holding back to give us that chance. It will not last for ever. We must take it or leave it.

BOOK III

Christian Behaviour

The Three Parts of Morality

THERE IS A STORY about a schoolboy who was asked what he thought God was like. He replied that, as far as he could make out, God was "The sort of person who is always snooping round to see if anyone is enjoying himself and then trying to stop it." And I am afraid that is the sort of idea that the word Morality raises in a good many people's minds: something that interferes, something that stops you having a good time. In reality, moral rules are directions for running the human machine. Every moral rule is there to prevent a breakdown, or a strain, or a friction, in the running of that machine. That is why these rules at first seem to be constantly interfering with our natural inclinations. When you are being taught how to use any machine, the instructor keeps on saying, "No, don't do it like that," because, of course, there are all sorts of things that look all right and seem to you the natural way of treating the machine, but do not really work.

Some people prefer to talk about moral "ideals" rather than moral rules and about moral "idealism" rather than moral obedience. Now it is, of course, quite true that moral perfection is an "ideal" in the sense that we cannot achieve it. In that sense every kind of perfection is, for us humans, an ideal; we cannot succeed in being perfect car drivers or perfect tennis players or in drawing perfectly straight lines. But there is another sense in which it is very misleading to call moral perfection an ideal. When a man says that a certain woman, or house, or ship, or garden is "his ideal" he does not mean (unless he is rather a fool) that everyone else ought to have the same ideal. In such matters we are entitled to have different tastes and, therefore, different ideals. But it is dangerous to describe a man who tries very hard to keep the moral law as a "man of high ideals," because this might lead you to think that moral perfection was a private taste of his own and that the rest of us were not called on to share it. This would be a disastrous mistake. Perfect behaviour may be as unattainable as perfect gear-changing when we drive; but it is a necessary ideal prescribed for all men by the very nature of the human machine just as perfect gear-changing is an ideal prescribed for all drivers by the very nature of cars. And it would be even more dangerous to think of oneself as a person "of high ideals" because one is trying to tell no lies at all (instead of only a few lies) or never to commit adultery (instead of committing it only seldom) or not to be a bully (instead of being only a moderate bully). It might lead you to become a prig and to think you were rather a special person who deserved to be congratulated on his "idealism." In reality you might just as well expect to be congratulated because, whenever you do a sum, you try to get it quite right. To be sure, perfect arithmetic is "an ideal"; you will certainly make some mistakes in some calculations. But there is nothing very fine about trying to be quite accurate at each step in each sum. It would be idiotic not to try; for every mistake is going to cause you trouble later on. In the same way every moral failure is going to cause trouble, probably to others and certainly to yourself. By talking about rules and obedience instead of "ideals" and "idealism" we help to remind ourselves of these facts.

Now let us go a step further. There are two ways in which the human machine goes wrong. One is when human individuals drift apart from one another, or else collide with one another and do one another damage, by cheating or bullying. The other is when things go wrong inside the individual— when the different parts of him (his different faculties and desires and so on) either drift apart or interfere with one another. You can get the idea plain if you think of us as a fleet of ships sailing in formation. The voyage will be a success only, in the first place, if the ships do not collide and get in one another's way; and, secondly, if each ship is seaworthy and has her engines in good order. As a matter of fact, you cannot have either of these two things without the other. If the ships keep on having collisions they will not remain seaworthy very long. On the other hand, if their steering gears are out of order they will not be able to avoid collisions. Or, if you like, think of humanity as a band playing a tune. To get a good result, you need two things. Each player's individual instrument must be in tune and also each must come in at the right moment so as to combine with all the others.

But there is one thing we have not yet taken into account. We have not asked where the fleet is trying to get to, or what piece of music the band is trying to play. The instruments might be all in tune and might all come in at the right moment, but even so the performance would not be a success if they had been engaged to provide dance music and actually played nothing but Dead Marches. And however well the fleet sailed, its voyage would be a failure if it were meant to reach New York and actually arrived at Calcutta.

Morality, then, seems to be concerned with three things. Firstly, with fair play and harmony between individuals. Secondly, with what might be called tidying up or harmonising the things inside each individual. Thirdly, with the general purpose of human life as a whole: what man was made for: what course the whole fleet ought to be on: what tune the conductor of the band wants it to play.

You may have noticed that modern people are nearly always thinking about the first thing and forgetting the other two. When people say in the newspapers that we are striving for

Christian moral standards, they usually mean that we are striving for kindness and fair play between nations, and classes, and individuals; that is, they are thinking only of the first thing. When a man says about something he wants to do, "It can't be wrong because it doesn't do anyone else any harm," he is thinking only of the first thing. He is thinking it does not matter what his ship is like inside provided that he does not run into the next ship. And it is quite natural, when we start thinking about morality, to begin with the first thing, with social relations. For one thing, the results of bad morality in that sphere are so obvious and press on us every day; war and poverty and graft and lies and shoddy work. And also, as long as you stick to the first thing, there is very little disagreement about morality. Almost all people at all times have agreed (in theory) that human beings ought to be honest and kind and helpful to one another. But though it is natural to begin with all that, if our thinking about morality stops there, we might just as well not have thought at all. Unless we go on to the second thing—the tidying up inside each human being—we are only deceiving ourselves.

What is the good of telling the ships how to steer so as to avoid collisions if, in fact, they are such crazy old tubs that they cannot be steered at all? What is the good of drawing up, on paper, rules for social behaviour, if we know that, in fact, our greed, cowardice, ill temper, and self-conceit are going to prevent us from keeping them? I do not mean for a moment that we ought not to think, and think hard, about improvements in our social and economic system. What I do mean is that all that thinking will be mere moonshine unless we realise that nothing but the courage and unselfishness of individuals is ever going to make any system work properly. It is easy enough to remove the particular kinds of graft or bullying that go on under the present system: but as long as men are twisters or bullies they will find some new way of carrying on the old game under the new system. You cannot make men good by law: and without good men you cannot have a good society. That is why we must go on to think of the second thing: of morality inside the individual.

But I do not think we can stop there either. We are now getting to the point at which different beliefs about the universe lead to different behaviour. And it would seem, at first sight, very sensible to stop before we got there, and just carry on with those parts of morality that all sensible people agree about. But can we? Remember that religion involves a series of statements about facts, which must be either true or false. If they are true, one set of conclusions will follow about the right sailing of the human fleet: if they are false, quite a different set. For example, let us go back to the man who says that a thing cannot be wrong unless it hurts some other human being. He quite understands that he must not damage the other ships in the convoy, but he honestly thinks that what he does to his own ship is simply his own business. But does it not make a great difference whether his ship is his own property or not? Does it not make a great difference whether I am, so to speak, the landlord of my own mind and body, or only a tenant, responsible to the real landlord? If somebody else made me, for his own purposes, then I shall have a lot of duties which I should not have if I simply belonged to myself.

Again, Christianity asserts that every individual human being is going to live for ever, and this must be either true or false. Now there are a good many things which would not be worth bothering about if I were going to live only seventy years, but which I had better bother about very seriously if I am going to live for ever. Perhaps my bad temper or my jealousy are gradually getting worse—so gradually that the increase in seventy years will not be very noticeable. But it might be absolute hell in a million years: in fact, if Christianity is true, Hell is the precisely correct technical term for what it would be. And immortality makes this other difference, which, by the by, has a connection with the difference between totalitarianism and democracy. If individuals live only seventy years, then a state, or a nation, or a civilisation, which may last for a thousand years, is more important than an individual. But if Christianity is true, then the individual is not only more important but incomparably more important, for he is everlasting and the life of a state or a civilisation, compared with his, is only a moment.

It seems, then, that if we are to think about morality, we must think of all three departments: relations between man and man: things inside each man: and relations between man and the power that made him. We can all co-operate in the first one. Disagreements begin with the second and become serious with the third. It is in dealing with the third that the main differences between Christian and non-Christian morality come out. For the rest of this book I am going to assume the Christian point of view, and look at the whole picture as it will be if Christianity is true.

CHAPTER 2

The "Cardinal Virtues"

THE PREVIOUS SECTION was originally composed to be given as a short talk on the air.

If you are allowed to talk for only ten minutes, pretty well everything else has to be sacrificed to brevity. One of my chief reasons for dividing morality up into three parts (with my picture of the ships sailing in convoy) was that this seemed the shortest way of covering the ground. Here I want to give some idea of another way in which the subject has been divided by old writers, which was too long to use in my talk, but which is a very good one.

According to this longer scheme there are seven "virtues." Four of them are called "Cardinal" virtues, and the remaining three are called "Theological" virtues. The "Cardinal" ones are those which all civilised people recognise: the "Theological" are those which, as a rule, only Christians know about. I shall deal with the Theological ones later on: at present I am talking about the four Cardinal virtues. (The word "cardinal" has nothing to do with "Cardinals" in the Roman Church. It comes from a Latin word meaning "the hinge of a door." These were called "cardinal" virtues because they are, as we should say, "pivotal.") They are PRUDENCE, TEMPERANCE, JUSTICE, and FORTITUDE.

Prudence means practical common sense, taking the trouble to think out what you are doing and what is likely to come of it. Nowadays most people hardly think of Prudence as one of the "virtues." In fact, because Christ said we could only get into His world by being like children, many Christians have the idea that, provided you are "good," it does not matter being a fool. But that is a misunderstanding. In the first place, most children show plenty of "prudence" about doing the things they are really interested in, and think them out quite sensibly. In the second place, as St. Paul points out, Christ never meant that we were to remain children in *intelligence*: on the contrary, He told us to be not only "as harmless as doves," but also "as wise as serpents." He wants a child's heart, but a grown-up's head. He wants us to be simple, single-minded, affectionate, and teachable, as good children are; but He also wants every bit of intelligence we have to be alert at its job, and in first-class fighting trim. The fact that you are giving money to a charity does not mean that you need not try to find out whether that charity is a fraud or not. The fact that what you are thinking about is God Himself (for example, when you are praying) does not mean that you can be content with the same babyish ideas which you had when you were a five-year-old. It is, of course, quite true that God will not love you any the less, or have less use for you, if you happen to have been born with a very second-rate brain. He has room for people with very little sense, but He wants every one to use what sense they have. The proper motto is not "Be good, sweet maid, and let who can be clever," but "Be good, sweet maid, and don't forget that this involves being as clever as you can." God is no fonder of intellectual slackers than of any other slackers. If you are thinking of becoming a Christian, I warn you, you are embarking on something which is going to take the whole of you, brains and all. But, fortunately, it works the other way round. Anyone who is honestly trying to be a Christian will soon find his intelligence being sharpened: one of the reasons why it needs no special education to be a Christian is that Christianity is an education itself. That is why an uneducated believer like Bunyan was able to write a book that has astonished the world.

Temperance is, unfortunately, one of those words that has changed its meaning. It now usually means teetotalism. But in the days when the second Cardinal virtue was christened "Temperance," it meant nothing of the sort. Temperance referred not specially to drink, but to all pleasures; and it meant not abstaining, but going the right length and no further. It is a mistake to think that Christians ought all to be teetotallers; Mohammedanism, not Christianity, is the teetotal religion. Of course it may be the duty of a particular Christian, or of any Christian, at a particular time, to abstain from strong drink, either because he is the sort of man who cannot drink at all without drinking too much, or because he wants to give the money to the poor, or because he is with people who are inclined to drunkenness and must not encourage them by drinking himself. But the whole point is that he is abstaining, for a good reason, from something which he does not condemn and which he likes to see other people enjoying. One of the marks of a certain type of bad man is that he cannot give up a thing himself without wanting every one else to give it up. That is not the Christian way. An individual Christian may see fit to give up all sorts of things for special reasons—marriage, or meat, or beer, or the cinema; but the moment he starts saying the things are bad in themselves, or looking down his nose at other people who do use them, he has taken the wrong turning.

One great piece of mischief has been done by the modern restriction of the word Temperance to the question of drink. It helps people to forget that you can be just as intemperate about lots of other things. A man who makes his golf or his motor-bicycle the centre of his life, or a woman who devotes all her thoughts to clothes or bridge or her dog, is being just as "intemperate" as someone who gets drunk every evening. Of course, it does not show on the outside so easily: bridge-mania or golf-mania do not make you fall down in the middle of the road. But God is not deceived by externals.

Justice means much more than the sort of thing that goes on in law courts. It is the old name for everything we should now call "fairness"; it includes honesty, give and take, truthfulness, keeping promises, and all that side of life. And Fortitude includes both kinds of courage—the kind that faces danger as well as the kind that "sticks it" under pain. "Guts" is perhaps the nearest modern English. You will notice, of course, that you cannot practise any of the other virtues very long without bringing this one into play.

There is one further point about the virtues that ought to be noticed. There is a difference between doing some particular just or temperate action and being a just or temperate man. Someone who is not a good tennis player may now and then make a good shot. What you mean by a good player is the man whose eye and muscles and nerves have been so trained by making innumerable good shots that they can now be relied on. They have a certain tone or quality which is there even when he is not playing, just as a mathematician's mind has a certain habit and outlook which is there even when he is not doing mathematics. In the same way a man who perseveres in doing just actions gets in the end a certain quality of character. Now it is that quality rather than the particular actions which we mean when we talk of "virtue."

This distinction is important for the following reason. If we thought only of the particular actions we might encourage three wrong ideas.

(1) We might think that, provided you did the right thing, it did not matter how or why you did it—whether you did it willingly or unwillingly, sulkily or cheerfully, through fear of public opinion or for its own sake. But the truth is that right actions done for the wrong reason do not help to build the internal quality or character called a "virtue," and it is this quality or character that really matters. (If the bad tennis player hits very hard, not because he sees that a very hard

stroke is required, but because he has lost his temper, his stroke might possibly, by luck, help him to win that particular game; but it will not be helping him to become a reliable player.)

(2) We might think that God wanted simply obedience to a set of rules: whereas He really wants people of a particular sort.

(3) We might think that the "virtues" were necessary only for this present life—that in the other world we could stop being just because there is nothing to quarrel about and stop being brave because there is no danger. Now it is quite true that there will probably be no occasion for just or courageous acts in the next world, but there will be every occasion for being the sort of people that we can become only as the result of doing such acts here. The point is not that God will refuse you admission to His eternal world if you have not got certain qualities of character: the point is that if people have not got at least the beginnings of those qualities inside them, then no possible external conditions could make a "Heaven" for them—that is, could make them happy with the deep, strong, unshakable kind of happiness God intends for us.

CHAPTER 3

Social Morality

THE FIRST THING TO GET CLEAR about Christian morality between man and man is that in this department Christ did not come to preach any brand new morality. The Golden Rule of the New Testament (Do as you would be done by) is a summing up of what everyone, at bottom, had always known to be right. Really great moral teachers never do introduce new moralities: it is quacks and cranks who do that. As Dr. Johnson said, "People need to be reminded more often than they need to be instructed." The real job of every moral teacher is to keep on bringing us back, time after time, to the old simple principles which we are all so anxious not to see; like bringing a horse back and back to the fence it has refused to jump or bringing a child back and back to the bit in its lesson that it wants to shirk.

The second thing to get clear is that Christianity has not, and does not profess to have, a detailed political programme for applying "Do as you would be done by" to a particular society at a particular moment. It could not have. It is meant for all men at all times and the particular programme which suited one place or time would not suit another. And, anyhow, that is not how Christianity works. When it tells you to feed the hungry it does not give you lessons in cookery. When it tells you to read the Scriptures it does not give you lessons in Hebrew and Greek, or even in English grammar. It was never intended to replace or supersede the ordinary human arts and sciences: it is rather a director which will set them all to the right jobs, and a source of energy which will give them all new life, if only they will put themselves at its disposal.

People say, "The Church ought to give us a lead." That is true if they mean it in the right way, but false if they mean it in the wrong way. By the Church they ought to mean the whole body of practising Christians. And when they say that the Church should give us a lead, they ought to mean that some Christians—those who happen to have the right talents—should be economists and statesmen, and that all economists and statesmen should be Christians, and that their whole efforts in politics and economics should be directed to putting "Do as you would be done by" into action. If that happened, and if we others were really ready to take it, then we should find the Christian solution for our own social problems pretty quickly. But, of course, when they ask for a lead from the Church most people mean they want the clergy to put out a political programme. That is silly. The clergy are those particular people within the whole Church who have been specially trained and set aside to look after what concerns us as creatures who are going to live for ever: and we are asking them to do a quite different job for which they have not been trained. The job is really on us, on the laymen. The application of Christian principles, say, to trade unionism or education, must come from Christian trade unionists and Christian schoolmasters: just as Christian literature comes from Christian novelists and dramatists—not from the bench of bishops getting together and trying to write plays and novels in their spare time.

All the same, the New Testament, without going into details, gives us a pretty clear hint of what a fully Christian society would be like. Perhaps it gives us more than we can take. It tells us that there are to be no passengers or parasites: if a man does not work, he ought not to eat. Every one is to work with his own hands, and what is more, every one's work is to produce something good: there will be no manufacture of silly luxuries and then of sillier advertisements to persuade us to buy them. And there is to be no "swank" or "side," no putting on airs. To that extent a Christian society would be what we now call Leftist. On the other hand, it is always insisting on obedience—obedience (and outward marks of respect) from all of us to properly appointed magistrates, from children to parents, and (I am afraid this is going to be very unpopular) from wives to husbands. Thirdly, it is to be a cheerful society full of singing and rejoicing, and regarding worry or anxiety as wrong. Courtesy is one of the Christian virtues; and the New Testament hates what it calls "busybodies."

If there were such a society in existence and you or I visited it, I think we should come away with a curious impression. We should feel that its economic life was very socialistic and, in that sense, "advanced," but that its family life and its code of manners were rather old-fashioned—perhaps even ceremonious and aristocratic. Each of us would like some bits of it, but I am afraid very few of us would like the whole thing. That is just what one would expect if Christianity is the total plan for the human machine. We have all departed from that total plan in different ways, and each of us wants to make out that his own modification of the original plan is the plan itself. You will find this again and again about anything that is really Christian: every one is attracted by bits of it and wants to pick out those bits and leave the rest. That is why we do not get much further: and that is why people who are fighting for quite opposite things can both say they are fighting for Christianity.

Now another point. There is one bit of advice given to us by the ancient heathen Greeks, and by the Jews in the Old Testament, and by the great Christian teachers of the Middle Ages, which the modern economic system has completely disobeyed. All these people told us not to lend money at interest and lending money at interest—what we call investment—is the basis of our whole system. Now it may not absolutely follow that we are wrong. Some people say that when Moses and Aristotle and the Christians agreed in forbidding interest (or "usury" as they called it), they could not foresee the joint stock company, and were only thinking of the private moneylender, and that, therefore, we need not bother about what they said. That is a question I cannot decide on. I am not an economist and I simply do not know whether the investment system is responsible for the state we are in or not. This is where we want the Christian economist. But I should not have been honest if I had not told you that three great civilisations had agreed (or so it seems at first sight) in condemning the very thing on which we have based our whole life.

One more point and I am done. In the passage where the New Testament says that every one must work, it gives as a reason "in order that he may have something to give to those in need." Charity—giving to the poor—is an essential part of Christian morality: in the frightening parable of the sheep and the goats it seems to be the point on which everything turns. Some people nowadays say that charity ought to be unnecessary and that instead of giving to the poor we ought to be producing a society in which there were no poor to give to. They may be quite right in saying that we ought to produce that kind of society. But if anyone thinks that, as a consequence, you can stop giving in the meantime, then he has parted company with all Christian morality. I do not believe one can settle how much we ought to give. I am afraid the only safe rule is to give more than we can spare. In other words, if our expenditure on comforts, luxuries, amusements, etc., is up to the standard common among those with the same income as our own, we are probably giving away too little. If our charities do not at all pinch or hamper us, I should say they are too small. There ought to be things we should like to do and cannot do because our charitable expenditure excludes them. I am speaking now of "charities" in the common way.

Particular cases of distress among your own relatives, friends, neighbours or employees, which God, as it were, forces upon your notice, may demand much more: even to the crippling and endangering of your own position. For many of us the great obstacle to charity lies not in our luxurious living or desire for more money, but in our fear—fear of insecurity. This must often be recognised as a temptation. Sometimes our pride also hinders our charity; we are tempted to spend more than we ought on the showy forms of generosity (tipping, hospitality) and less than we ought on those who really need our help.

And now, before I end, I am going to venture on a guess as to how this section has affected any who have read it. My guess is that there are some Leftist people among them who are very angry that it has not gone further in that direction, and some people of an opposite sort who are angry because they think it has gone much too far. If so, that brings us right up against the real snag in all this drawing up of blueprints for a Christian society. Most of us are not really approaching the subject in order to find out what Christianity says: we are approaching it in the hope of finding support from Christianity for the views of our own party. We are looking for an ally where we are offered either a Master or—a Judge. I am just the same. There are bits in this section that I wanted to leave out. And that is why nothing whatever is going to come of such talks unless we go a much longer way round. A Christian society is not going to arrive until most of us really want it: and we are not going to want it until we become fully Christian. I may repeat "Do as you would be done by" till I am black in the face, but I cannot really carry it out till I love my neighbour as myself: and I cannot learn to love my neighbour as myself till I learn to love God: and I cannot learn to love God except by learning to obey Him. And so, as I warned you, we are driven on to something more inward—driven on from social matters to religious matters. For the longest way round is the shortest way home.

CHAPTER 4
Morality and Psychoanalysis

❀

I HAVE SAID that we should never get a Christian society unless most of us became Christian individuals. That does not
mean, of course, that we can put off doing anything about
society until some imaginary date in the far future. It means
that we must begin both jobs at once—(1) the job of seeing
how "Do as you would be done by" can be applied in detail
to modern society, and (2) the job of becoming the sort of people who really would apply it if we saw how. I now want to
begin considering what the Christian idea of a good man is—
the Christian specification for the human machine.

Before I come down to details there are two more general
points I should like to make. First of all, since Christian morality claims to be a technique for putting the human machine
right, I think you would like to know how it is related to another technique which seems to make a similar claim—
namely, psychoanalysis.

Now you want to distinguish very clearly between two
things: between the actual medical theories and technique of
the psychoanalysts, and the general philosophical view of the
world which Freud and some others have gone on to add to
this. The second thing—the philosophy of Freud—is in direct
contradiction to Christianity; and also in direct contradiction

to the other great psychologist, Jung. And furthermore, when Freud is talking about how to cure neurotics he is speaking as a specialist on his own subject, but when he goes on to talk general philosophy he is speaking as an amateur. It is therefore quite sensible to attend to him with respect in the one case and not in the other—and that is what I do. I am all the readier to do it because I have found that when he is talking off his own subject and on a subject I do know something about (namely, languages) he is very ignorant. But psychoanalysis itself, apart from all the philosophical additions that Freud and others have made to it, is not in the least contradictory to Christianity. Its technique overlaps with Christian morality at some points and it would not be a bad thing if every parson knew something about it: but it does not run the same course all the way, for the two techniques are doing rather different things.

When a man makes a moral choice two things are involved. One is the act of choosing. The other is the various feelings, impulses and so on which his psychological outfit presents him with, and which are the raw material of his choice. Now this raw material may be of two kinds. Either it may be what we would call normal: it may consist of the sort of feelings that are common to all men. Or else it may consist of quite unnatural feelings due to things that have gone wrong in his subconscious. Thus fear of things that are really dangerous would be an example of the first kind: an irrational fear of cats or spiders would be an example of the second kind. The desire of a man for a woman would be of the first kind: the perverted desire of a man for a man would be of the second. Now what psychoanalysis undertakes to do is to remove the abnormal feelings, that is, to give the man better raw material for his acts of choice: morality is concerned with the acts of choice themselves.

Put it this way. Imagine three men who go to war. One has the ordinary natural fear of danger that any man has and he subdues it by moral effort and becomes a brave man. Let us suppose that the other two have, as a result of things in their subconsciousness, exaggerated, irrational fears, which no amount of moral effort can do anything about. Now suppose that a psychoanalyst comes along and cures these two: that is, he puts them both back in the position of the first man. Well it is just then that the psychoanalytical problem is over and the moral problem begins. Because, now that they are cured, these two men might take quite different lines. The first might say, "Thank goodness I've got rid of all those doo-dahs. Now at last I can do what I always wanted to do—my duty to the cause of freedom." But the other might say, "Well, I'm very glad that I now feel moderately cool under fire, but, of course, that doesn't alter the fact that I'm still jolly well determined to look after Number One and let the other chap do the dangerous job whenever I can. Indeed one of the good things about feeling less frightened is that I can now look after myself much more efficiently and can be much cleverer at hiding the fact from the others." Now this difference is a purely moral one and psychoanalysis cannot do anything about it. However much you improve the man's raw material, you have still got something else: the real, free choice of the man, on the material presented to him, either to put his own advantage first or to put it last. And this free choice is the only thing that morality is concerned with.

The bad psychological material is not a sin but a disease. It does not need to be repented of, but to be cured. And by the way, that is very important. Human beings judge one another by their external actions. God judges them by their moral choices. When a neurotic who has a pathological horror of cats forces himself to pick up a cat for some good reason, it is quite possible that in God's eyes he has shown more courage than a healthy man may have shown in winning the V.C. When a man who has been perverted from his youth and taught that cruelty is the right thing, does some tiny little kindness, or refrains from some cruelty he might have committed, and thereby, perhaps, risks being sneered at by his companions, he may, in God's eyes, be doing more than you and I would do if we gave up life itself for a friend.

It is as well to put this the other way round. Some of us who seem quite nice people may, in fact, have made so little use of a good heredity and a good upbringing that we are really worse than those whom we regard as fiends. Can we be quite certain how we should have behaved if we had been saddled with the psychological outfit, and then with the bad upbringing, and then with the power, say, of Himmler? That is why Christians are told not to judge. We see only the results which a man's choices make out of his raw material. But God does not judge him on the raw material at all, but on what he has done with it. Most of the man's psychological make-up is probably due to his body: when his body dies all that will fall off him, and the real central man, the thing that chose, that made the best or the worst out of this material, will stand naked. All sorts of nice things which we thought our own, but which were really due to a good digestion, will fall off some of us: all sorts of nasty things which were due to complexes or bad health will fall off others. We shall then, for the first time, see every one as he really was. There will be surprises.

And that leads on to my second point. People often think of Christian morality as a kind of bargain in which God says, "If you keep a lot of rules I'll reward you, and if you don't I'll do the other thing." I do not think that is the best way of looking at it. I would much rather say that every time you make a choice you are turning the central part of you, the part of you that chooses, into something a little different from what it was before. And taking your life as a whole, with all your innumerable choices, all your life long you are slowly turning this central thing either into a heavenly creature or into a hellish creature: either into a creature that is in harmony with God, and with other creatures, and with itself, or else into one that is in a state of war and hatred with God, and with its fellow-creatures, and with itself. To be the one kind of creature is heaven: that is, it is joy and peace and knowledge and power.

To be the other means madness, horror, idiocy, rage, impotence, and eternal loneliness. Each of us at each moment is progressing to the one state or the other.

That explains what always used to puzzle me about Christian writers; they seem to be so very strict at one moment and so very free and easy at another. They talk about mere sins of thought as if they were immensely important: and then they talk about the most frightful murders and treacheries as if you had only got to repent and all would be forgiven. But I have come to see that they are right. What they are always thinking of is the mark which the action leaves on that tiny central self which no one sees in this life but which each of us will have to endure—or enjoy—for ever. One man may be so placed that his anger sheds the blood of thousands, and another so placed that however angry he gets he will only be laughed at. But the little mark on the soul may be much the same in both. Each has done something to himself which, unless he repents, will make it harder for him to keep out of the rage next time he is tempted, and will make the rage worse when he does fall into it. Each of them, if he seriously turns to God, can have that twist in the central man straightened out again: each is, in the long run, doomed if he will not. The bigness or smallness of the thing, seen from the outside, is not what really matters.

One last point. Remember that, as I said, the right direction leads not only to peace but to knowledge. When a man is getting better he understands more and more clearly the evil that is still left in him. When a man is getting worse, he understands his own badness less and less. A moderately bad man knows he is not very good: a thoroughly bad man thinks he is all right. This is common sense, really. You understand sleep when you are awake, not while you are sleeping. You can see mistakes in arithmetic when your mind is working properly: while you are making them you cannot see them. You can understand the nature of drunkenness when you are sober, not when you are drunk. Good people know about both good and evil: bad people do not know about either.

CHAPTER 5
Sexual Morality

❋

We must now consider Christian morality as regards sex, what Christians call the virtue of chastity. The Christian rule of chastity must not be confused with the social rule of "modesty" (in one sense of that word); i.e. propriety, or decency. The social rule of propriety lays down how much of the human body should be displayed and what subjects can be referred to, and in what words, according to the customs of a given social circle. Thus, while the rule of chastity is the same for all Christians at all times, the rule of propriety changes. A girl in the Pacific islands wearing hardly any clothes and a Victorian lady completely covered in clothes might both be equally "modest," proper, or decent, according to the standards of their own societies: and both, for all we could tell by their dress, might be equally chaste (or equally unchaste). Some of the language which chaste women used in Shakespeare's time would have been used in the nineteenth century only by a woman completely abandoned. When people break the rule of propriety current in their own time and place, if they do so in order to excite lust in themselves or others, then they are offending against chastity. But if they break it through ignorance or carelessness they are guilty only of bad manners. When, as often happens, they break it defiantly in order to shock or embarrass others, they are not necessarily being un-chaste, but they are being uncharitable: for it is uncharitable to take pleasure in making other people uncomfortable. I do not think that a very strict or fussy standard of propriety is any proof of chastity or any help to it, and I therefore regard the great relaxation and simplifying of the rule which has taken place in my own lifetime as a good thing. At its present stage, however, it has this inconvenience, that people of dif-ferent ages and different types do not all acknowledge the same standard, and we hardly know where we are. While this confusion lasts I think that old, or old-fashioned, people should be very careful not to assume that young or "emanci-pated" people are corrupt whenever they are (by the old stan-dard) improper; and, in return, that young people should not call their elders prudes or puritans because they do not easily adopt the new standard. A real desire to believe all the good you can of others and to make others as comfortable as you can will solve most of the problems.

Chastity is the most unpopular of the Christian virtues. There is no getting away from it: the old Christian rule is, "Either marriage, with complete faithfulness to your partner, or else total abstinence." Now this is so difficult and so con-trary to our instincts, that obviously either Christianity is wrong or our sexual instinct, as it now is, has gone wrong. One or the other. Of course, being a Christian, I think it is the instinct which has gone wrong.

But I have other reasons for thinking so. The biological pur-pose of sex is children, just as the biological purpose of eating is to repair the body. Now if we eat whenever we feel inclined and just as much as we want, it is quite true that most of us will eat too much: but not terrifically too much. One man may eat enough for two, but he does not eat enough for ten. The appetite goes a little beyond its biological purpose, but not enormously. But if a healthy young man indulged his sexual appetite whenever he felt inclined, and if each act produced a baby, then in ten years he might easily populate a small village. This appetite is in ludicrous and preposterous excess of its function.

Or take it another way. You can get a large audience together for a strip-tease act—that is, to watch a girl undress on the stage. Now suppose you came to a country where you could fill a theatre by simply bringing a covered plate on to the stage and then slowly lifting the cover so as to let every one see, just before the lights went out, that it contained a mutton chop or a bit of bacon, would you not think that in that country something had gone wrong with the appetite for food? And would not anyone who had grown up in a different world think there was something equally queer about the state of the sex instinct among us?

One critic said that if he found a country in which such strip-tease acts with food were popular, he would conclude that the people of that country were starving. He meant, of course, to imply that such things as the strip-tease act resulted not from sexual corruption but from sexual starvation. I agree with him that if, in some strange land, we found that similar acts with mutton chops were popular, one of the possible explanations which would occur to me would be famine. But the next step would be to test our hypothesis by finding out whether, in fact, much or little food was being consumed in that country. If the evidence showed that a good deal was being eaten, then of course we should have to abandon the hypothesis of starvation and try to think of another one. In the same way, before accepting sexual starvation as the cause of the strip-tease, we should have to look for evidence that there is in fact more sexual abstinence in our age than in those ages when things like the strip-tease were unknown. But surely there is no such evidence. Contraceptives have made sexual indulgence far less costly within marriage and far safer outside it than ever before, and public opinion is less hostile to illicit unions and even to perversion than it has been since Pagan times. Nor is the hypothesis of "starvation" the only one we can imagine. Everyone knows that the sexual appetite, like our other appetites, grows by indulgence. Starving men may think much about food, but so do gluttons; the gorged, as well as the famished, like titillations.

Here is a third point. You find very few people who want to eat things that really are not food or to do other things with food instead of eating it. In other words, perversions of the food appetite are rare. But perversions of the sex instinct are numerous, hard to cure, and frightful. I am sorry to have to go into all these details, but I must. The reason why I must is that you and I, for the last twenty years, have been fed all day long on good solid lies about sex. We have been told, till one is sick of hearing it, that sexual desire is in the same state as any of our other natural desires and that if only we abandon the silly old Victorian idea of hushing it up, everything in the garden will be lovely. It is not true. The moment you look at the facts, and away from the propaganda, you see that it is not.

They tell you sex has become a mess because it was hushed up. But for the last twenty years it has not been hushed up. It has been chattered about all day long. Yet it is still in a mess. If hushing up had been the cause of the trouble, ventilation would have set it right. But it has not. I think it is the other way round. I think the human race originally hushed it up because it had become such a mess. Modern people are always saying, "Sex is nothing to be ashamed of." They may mean two things. They may mean "There is nothing to be ashamed of in the fact that the human race reproduces itself in a certain way, nor in the fact that it gives pleasure." If they mean that, they are right. Christianity says the same. It is not the thing, nor the pleasure, that is the trouble. The old Christian teachers said that if man had never fallen, sexual pleasure, instead of being less than it is now, would actually have been greater. I know some muddle-headed Christians have talked as if Christianity thought that sex, or the body, or pleasure, were bad in themselves. But they were wrong. Christianity is almost the only one of the great religions which thoroughly approves of the body—which believes that matter is good, that God Him-

self once took on a human body, that some kind of body is
going to be given to us even in Heaven and is going to be an
essential part of our happiness, our beauty, and our energy
Christianity has glorified marriage more than any other religion: and nearly all the greatest love poetry in the world has
been produced by Christians. If anyone says that sex, in itself
is bad, Christianity contradicts him at once. But, of course
when people say, "Sex is nothing to be ashamed of," they may
mean "the state into which the sexual instinct has now got is
nothing to be ashamed of."

If they mean that, I think they are wrong. I think it is everything to be ashamed of. There is nothing to be ashamed of in
enjoying your food: there would be everything to be ashamed
of if half the world made food the main interest of their lives
and spent their time looking at pictures of food and dribbling
and smacking their lips. I do not say you and I are individually responsible for the present situation. Our ancestors have
handed over to us organisms which are warped in this respect:
and we grow up surrounded by propaganda in favour of unchastity. There are people who want to keep our sex instinct
inflamed in order to make money out of us. Because, of
course, a man with an obsession is a man who has very little
sales-resistance. God knows our situation; He will not judge
us as if we had no difficulties to overcome. What matters is
the sincerity and perseverance of our will to overcome them.

Before we can be cured we must want to be cured. Those
who really wish for help will get it; but for many modern people even the wish is difficult. It is easy to think that we want
something when we do not really want it. A famous Christian
long ago told us that when he was a young man he prayed
constantly for chastity; but years later he realised that while
his lips had been saying, "Oh Lord, make me chaste," his
heart had been secretly adding, "But please don't do it just
yet." This may happen in prayers for other virtues too; but
there are three reasons why it is now specially difficult for us
to desire—let alone to achieve—complete chastity.

In the first place our warped natures, the devils who tempt us, and all the contemporary propaganda for lust, combine to make us feel that the desires we are resisting are so "natural," so "healthy," and so reasonable, that it is almost perverse and abnormal to resist them. Poster after poster, film after film, novel after novel, associate the idea of sexual indulgence with the ideas of health, normality, youth, frankness, and good humour. Now this association is a lie. Like all powerful lies, it is based on a truth—the truth, acknowledged above, that sex in itself (apart from the excesses and obsessions that have grown round it) is "normal" and "healthy," and all the rest of it. The lie consists in the suggestion that any sexual act to which you are tempted at the moment is also healthy and normal. Now this, on any conceivable view, and quite apart from Christianity, must be nonsense. Surrender to all our desires obviously leads to impotence, disease, jealousies, lies, concealment, and everything that is the reverse of health, good humour, and frankness. For any happiness, even in this world, quite a lot of restraint is going to be necessary; so the claim made by every desire, when it is strong, to be healthy and reasonable, counts for nothing. Every sane and civilised man must have some set of principles by which he chooses to reject some of his desires and to permit others. One man does this on Christian principles, another on hygienic principles, another on sociological principles. The real conflict is not between Christianity and "nature," but between Christian principles and other principles in the control of "nature." For "nature" (in the sense of natural desire) will have to be controlled anyway, unless you are going to ruin your whole life. The Christian principles are, admittedly, stricter than the others; but then we think you will get help towards obeying them which you will not get towards obeying the others.

In the second place, many people are deterred from seriously attempting Christian chastity because they think (before trying) that it is impossible. But when a thing has to be attempted, one must never think about possibility or impossibility. Faced with an optional question in an examination paper, one considers whether one can do it or not: faced with a compulsory question, one must do the best one can. You may get some marks for a very imperfect answer: you will certainly get none for leaving the question alone. Not only in examinations but in war, in mountain climbing, in learning to skate, or swim, or ride a bicycle, even in fastening a stiff collar with cold fingers, people quite often do what seemed impossible before they did it. It is wonderful what you can do when you have to.

We may, indeed, be sure that perfect chastity—like perfect charity—will not be attained by any merely human efforts. You must ask for God's help. Even when you have done so, it may seem to you for a long time that no help, or less help than you need, is being given. Never mind. After each failure, ask forgiveness, pick yourself up, and try again. Very often what God first helps us towards is not the virtue itself but just this power of always trying again. For however important chastity (or courage, or truthfulness, or any other virtue) may be, this process trains us in habits of the soul which are more important still. It cures our illusions about ourselves and teaches us to depend on God. We learn, on the one hand, that we cannot trust ourselves even in our best moments, and, on the other, that we need not despair even in our worst, for our failures are forgiven. The only fatal thing is to sit down content with anything less than perfection.

Thirdly, people often misunderstand what psychology teaches about "repressions." It teaches us that "repressed" sex is dangerous. But "repressed" is here a technical term: it does not mean "suppressed" in the sense of "denied" or "resisted." A repressed desire or thought is one which has been thrust into the subconscious (usually at a very early age) and can now come before the mind only in a disguised and unrecognisable form. Repressed sexuality does not appear to the patient to be sexuality at all. When an adolescent or an adult is engaged in resisting a conscious desire, he is not dealing with a repression nor is he in the least danger of creating a repression. On the contrary, those who are seriously attempting chastity are more conscious, and soon know a great deal more about their own sexuality than anyone else. They come to know their desires as Wellington knew Napoleon, or as Sherlock Holmes knew Moriarty; as a rat-catcher knows rats or a plumber knows about leaky pipes. Virtue—even attempted virtue—brings light; indulgence brings fog.

Finally, though I have had to speak at some length about sex, I want to make it as clear as I possibly can that the centre of Christian morality is not here. If anyone thinks that Christians regard unchastity as the supreme vice, he is quite wrong. The sins of the flesh are bad, but they are the least bad of all sins. All the worst pleasures are purely spiritual: the pleasure of putting other people in the wrong, of bossing and patronising and spoiling sport, and back-biting; the pleasures of power, of hatred. For there are two things inside me, competing with the human self which I must try to become. They are the Animal self, and the Diabolical self. The Diabolical self is the worse of the two. That is why a cold, self-righteous prig who goes regularly to church may be far nearer to hell than a prostitute. But, of course, it is better to be neither.

CHAPTER 6
Christian Marriage

THE LAST CHAPTER was mainly negative. I discussed what was wrong with the sexual impulse in man, but said very little about its right working—in other words, about Christian marriage. There are two reasons why I do not particularly want to deal with marriage. The first is that the Christian doctrines on this subject are extremely unpopular. The second is that I have never been married myself, and, therefore, can speak only at second hand. But in spite of that, I feel I can hardly leave the subject out in an account of Christian morals.

The Christian idea of marriage is based on Christ's words that a man and wife are to be regarded as a single organism—for that is what the words "one flesh" would be in modern English. And the Christians believe that when He said this He was not expressing a sentiment but stating a fact—just as one is stating a fact when one says that a lock and its key are one mechanism, or that a violin and a bow are one musical instrument. The inventor of the human machine was telling us that its two halves, the male and the female, were made to be combined together in pairs, not simply on the sexual level, but totally combined. The monstrosity of sexual intercourse outside marriage is that those who indulge in it are trying to isolate one kind of union (the sexual) from all the other kinds of

88

union which were intended to go along with it and make up the total union. The Christian attitude does not mean that there is anything wrong about sexual pleasure, any more than about the pleasure of eating. It means that you must not isolate that pleasure and try to get it by itself, any more than you ought to try to get the pleasures of taste without swallowing and digesting, by chewing things and spitting them out again.

As a consequence, Christianity teaches that marriage is for life. There is, of course, a difference here between different Churches: some do not admit divorce at all; some allow it reluctantly in very special cases. It is a great pity that Christians should disagree about such a question; but for an ordinary layman the thing to notice is that Churches all agree with one another about marriage a great deal more than any of them agrees with the outside world. I mean, they all regard divorce as something like cutting up a living body, as a kind of surgical operation. Some of them think the operation so violent that it cannot be done at all; others admit it as a desperate remedy in extreme cases. They are all agreed that it is more like having both your legs cut off than it is like dissolving a business partnership or even deserting a regiment. What they all disagree with is the modern view that it is a simple readjustment of partners, to be made whenever people feel they are no longer in love with one another, or when either of them falls in love with someone else.

Before we consider this modern view in its relation to chastity, we must not forget to consider it in relation to another virtue, namely justice. Justice, as I said before, includes the keeping of promises. Now everyone who has been married in a church has made a public, solemn promise to stick to his (or her) partner till death. The duty of keeping that promise has no special connection with sexual morality: it is in the same position as any other promise. If, as modern people are always telling us, the sexual impulse is just like all our other impulses, then it ought to be treated like all our other impulses; and as their indulgence is controlled by our promises, so should its be. If, as I think, it is not like all our other impulses, but is morbidly inflamed, then we should be especially careful not to let it lead us into dishonesty.

To this someone may reply that he regarded the promise made in church as a mere formality and never intended to keep it. Whom, then, was he trying to deceive when he made it? God? That was really very unwise. Himself? That was not very much wiser. The bride, or bridegroom, or the "in-laws"? That was treacherous. Most often, I think, the couple (or one of them) hoped to deceive the public. They wanted the respectability that is attached to marriage without intending to pay the price: that is, they were imposters, they cheated. If they are still contented cheats, I have nothing to say to them: who would urge the high and hard duty of chastity on people who have not yet wished to be merely honest? If they have now come to their senses and want to be honest, their promise, already made, constrains them. And this, you will see, comes under the heading of justice, not that of chastity. If people do not believe in permanent marriage, it is perhaps better that they should live together unmarried than that they should make vows they do not mean to keep. It is true that by living together without marriage they will be guilty (in Christian eyes) of fornication. But one fault is not mended by adding another: unchastity is not improved by adding perjury.

The idea that "being in love" is the only reason for remaining married really leaves no room for marriage as a contract or promise at all. If love is the whole thing, then the promise can add nothing; and if it adds nothing, then it should not be made. The curious thing is that lovers themselves, while they remain really in love, know this better than those who talk about love. As Chesterton pointed out, those who are in love have a natural inclination to bind themselves by promises. Love songs all over the world are full of vows of eternal constancy. The Christian law is not forcing upon the passion of love something which is foreign to that passion's own nature: it is demanding that lovers should take seriously something which their passion of itself impels them to do.

And, of course, the promise, made when I am in love and because I am in love, to be true to the beloved as long as I live, commits one to being true even if I cease to be in love. A promise must be about things that I can do, about actions: no one can promise to go on feeling in a certain way. He might as well promise never to have a headache or always to feel hungry. But what, it may be asked, is the use of keeping two people together if they are no longer in love? There are several sound, social reasons; to provide a home for their children, to protect the woman (who has probably sacrificed or damaged her own career by getting married) from being dropped whenever the man is tired of her. But there is also another reason of which I am very sure, though I find it a little hard to explain.

It is hard because so many people cannot be brought to realise that when B is better than C, A may be even better than B. They like thinking in terms of good and bad, not of good, better, and best, or bad, worse and worst. They want to know whether you think patriotism a good thing: if you reply that it is, of course, far better than individual selfishness, but that it is inferior to universal charity and should always give way to universal charity when the two conflict, they think you are being evasive. They ask what you think of duelling. If you reply that it is far better to forgive a man than to fight a duel with him, but that even a duel might be better than a lifelong enmity which expresses itself in secret efforts to "do the man down," they go away complaining that you would not give them a straight answer. I hope no one will make this mistake about what I am now going to say.

What we call "being in love" is a glorious state, and, in several ways, good for us. It helps to make us generous and courageous, it opens our eyes not only to the beauty of the beloved but to all beauty, and it subordinates (especially at first) our merely animal sexuality; in that sense, love is the great conqueror of lust. No one in his senses would deny that being in love is far better than either common sensuality or cold self-centredness. But, as I said before, "the most dangerous thing you can do is to take any one impulse of our own nature and set it up as the thing you ought to follow at all costs." Being in love is a good thing, but it is not the best thing. There are many things below it, but there are also things above it. You cannot make it the basis of a whole life. It is a noble feeling, but it is still a feeling. Now no feeling can be relied on to last in its full intensity, or even to last at all. Knowledge can last, principles can last, habits can last; but feelings come and go. And in fact, whatever people say, the state called "being in love" usually does not last. If the old fairy-tale ending "They lived happily ever after" is taken to mean "They felt for the next fifty years exactly as they felt the day before they were married," then it says what probably never was nor ever could be true, and would be highly undesirable if it were. Who could bear to live in that excitement for even five years? What would become of your work, your appetite, your sleep, your friendships? But, of course, ceasing to be "in love" need not mean ceasing to love. Love in this second sense—love as distinct from "being in love" is not merely a feeling. It is a deep unity, maintained by the will and deliberately strengthened by habit; reinforced by (in Christian marriages) the grace which both partners ask, and receive, from God. They can have this love for each other even at those moments when they do not like each other; as you love yourself even when you do not like yourself. They can retain this love even when each would easily, if they allowed themselves, be "in love" with someone else. "Being in love" first moved them to promise fidelity: this quieter love enables them to keep the promise. It is on this love that the engine of marriage is run: being in love was the explosion that started it.

If you disagree with me, of course, you will say, "He knows nothing about it, he is not married." You may quite possibly be right. But before you say that, make quite sure that you are judging me by what you really know from your own experience and from watching the lives of your friends, and not by ideas you have derived from novels and films. This is not so easy to do as people think. Our experience is coloured through and through by books and plays and the cinema, and it takes patience and skill to disentangle the things we have really learned from life for ourselves.

People get from books the idea that if you have married the right person you may expect to go on "being in love" for ever. As a result, when they find they are not, they think this proves they have made a mistake and are entitled to a change—not realising that, when they have changed, the glamour will presently go out of the new love just as it went out of the old one. In this department of life, as in every other, thrills come at the beginning and do not last. The sort of thrill a boy has at the first idea of flying will not go on when he has joined the R.A.F. and is really learning to fly. The thrill you feel on first seeing some delightful place dies away when you really go to live there. Does this mean it would be better not to learn to fly and not to live in the beautiful place? By no means. In both cases, if you go through with it, the dying away of the first thrill will be compensated for by a quieter and more lasting kind of interest. What is more (and I can hardly find words to tell you how important I think this), it is just the people who are ready to submit to the loss of the thrill and settle down to the sober interest, who are then most likely to meet new thrills in some quite different direction. The man who has learned to fly and becomes a good pilot will suddenly discover music; the man who has settled down to live in the beauty spot will discover gardening.

This is, I think, one little part of what Christ meant by saying that a thing will not really live unless it first dies. It is simply no good trying to keep any thrill: that is the very worst thing you can do. Let the thrill go—let it die away—go on through that period of death into the quieter interest and happiness that follow—and you will find you are living in a world of new thrills all the time. But if you decide to make thrills your regular diet and try to prolong them artificially, they will all get weaker and weaker, and fewer and fewer, and you will be a bored, disillusioned old man for the rest of your life. It is because so few people understand this that you find many middle-aged men and women maundering about their lost youth, at the very age when new horizons ought to be appearing and new doors opening all around them. It is much better fun to learn to swim than to go on endlessly (and hopelessly) trying to get back the feeling you had when you first went paddling as a small boy.

Another notion we get from novels and plays is that "falling in love" is something quite irresistible; something that just happens to one, like measles. And because they believe this, some married people throw up the sponge and give in when they find themselves attracted by a new acquaintance. But I am inclined to think that these irresistible passions are much rarer in real life than in books, at any rate when one is grown up. When we meet someone beautiful and clever and sympathetic, of course we ought, in one sense, to admire and love these good qualities. But is it not very largely in our own choice whether this love shall, or shall not, turn into what we call "being in love"? No doubt, if our minds are full of novels and plays and sentimental songs, and our bodies full of alcohol, we shall turn any love we feel into that kind of love: just as if you have a rut in your path all the rainwater will run into that rut, and if you wear blue spectacles everything you see will turn blue. But that will be our own fault.

Before leaving the question of divorce, I should like to distinguish two things which are very often confused. The Christian conception of marriage is one: the other is the quite different question—how far Christians, if they are voters or Members of Parliament, ought to try to force their views of marriage on the rest of the community by embodying them in the divorce laws. A great many people seem to think that if you are a Christian yourself you should try to make divorce difficult for every one. I do not think that. At least I know I should be very angry if the Mohammedans tried to prevent the rest of us from drinking wine. My own view is that the

Churches should frankly recognise that the majority of the British people are not Christians and, therefore, cannot be expected to live Christian lives. There ought to be two distinct kinds of marriage: one governed by the State with rules enforced on all citizens, the other governed by the Church with rules enforced by her on her own members. The distinction ought to be quite sharp, so that a man knows which couples are married in a Christian sense and which are not.

So much for the Christian doctrine about the permanence of marriage. Something else, even more unpopular, remains to be dealt with. Christian wives promise to obey their husbands. In Christian marriage the man is said to be the "head." Two questions obviously arise here (1) Why should there be a head at all—why not equality? (2) Why should it be the man?

(1) The need for some head follows from the idea that marriage is permanent. Of course, as long as the husband and wife are agreed, no question of a head need arise; and we may hope that this will be the normal state of affairs in a Christian marriage. But when there is a real disagreement, what is to happen? Talk it over, of course; but I am assuming they have done that and still failed to reach agreement. What do they do next? They cannot decide by a majority vote, for in a council of two there can be no majority. Surely, only one or other of two things can happen: either they must separate and go their own ways or else one or other of them must have a casting vote. If marriage is permanent, one or other party must, in the last resort, have the power of deciding the family policy. You cannot have a permanent association without a constitution.

(2) If there must be a head, why the man? Well, firstly, is there any very serious wish that it should be the woman? As I have said, I am not married myself, but as far as I can see, even a woman who wants to be the head of her own house does not usually admire the same state of things when she finds it going on next door. She is much more likely to say "Poor Mr. X! Why he allows that appalling woman to boss him about the way she does is more than I can imagine." I do

not think she is even very flattered if anyone mentions the fact of her own "headship." There must be something unnatural about the rule of wives over husbands, because the wives themselves are half ashamed of it and despise the husbands whom they rule. But there is also another reason; and here I speak quite frankly as a bachelor, because it is a reason you can see from outside even better than from inside. The relations of the family to the outer world—what might be called its foreign policy—must depend, in the last resort, upon the man, because he always ought to be, and usually is, much more just to the outsiders. A woman is primarily fighting for her own children and husband against the rest of the world. Naturally, almost, in a sense, rightly, their claims override, for her, all other claims. She is the special trustee of their interests. The function of the husband is to see that this natural preference of hers is not given its head. He has the last word in order to protect other people from the intense family patriotism of the wife. If anyone doubts this, let me ask a simple question. If your dog has bitten the child next door, or if your child has hurt the dog next door, which would you sooner have to deal with, the master of that house or the mistress? Or, if you are a married woman, let me ask you this question. Much as you admire your husband, would you not say that his chief failing is his tendency not to stick up for his rights and yours against the neighbours as vigorously as you would like? A bit of an Appeaser?

CHAPTER 7

Forgiveness

❋

I SAID IN A PREVIOUS CHAPTER that chastity was the most unpopular of the Christian virtues. But I am not sure I was right. I believe the one I have to talk of today is even more unpopular: the Christian rule, "Thou shalt love thy neighbour as thyself." Because in Christian morals "thy neighbour" includes "thy enemy," and so we come up against this terrible duty of forgiving our enemies.

Every one says forgiveness is a lovely idea, until they have something to forgive, as we had during the war. And then, to mention the subject at all is to be greeted with howls of anger. It is not that people think this too high and difficult a virtue: it is that they think it hateful and contemptible. "That sort of talk makes them sick," they say. And half of you already want to ask me, "I wonder how you'd feel about forgiving the Gestapo if you were a Pole or a Jew?"

So do I. I wonder very much. Just as when Christianity tells me that I must not deny my religion even to save myself from death by torture, I wonder very much what I should do when it came to the point. I am not trying to tell you in this book what I could do—I can do precious little—I am telling you what Christianity is. I did not invent it. And there, right in the middle of it, I find "Forgive us our sins as we forgive those that sin against us." There is no slightest suggestion that we are offered forgiveness on any other terms. It is made perfectly clear that if we do not forgive we shall not be forgiven. There are no two ways about it. What are we to do?

It is going to be hard enough, anyway, but I think there are two things we can do to make it easier. When you start mathematics you do not begin with the calculus; you begin with simple addition. In the same way, if we really want (but all depends on really wanting) to learn how to forgive, perhaps we had better start with something easier than the Gestapo. One might start with forgiving one's husband or wife, or parents or children, or the nearest N.C.O., for something they have done or said in the last week. That will probably keep us busy for the moment. And secondly, we might try to understand exactly what loving your neighbour as yourself means. I have to love him as I love myself. Well, how exactly do I love myself?

Now that I come to think of it, I have not exactly got a feeling of fondness or affection for myself, and I do not even always enjoy my own society. So apparently "Love your neighbour" does not mean "feel fond of him" or "find him attractive." I ought to have seen that before, because, of course, you cannot feel fond of a person by trying. Do I think well of myself, think myself a nice chap? Well, I am afraid I sometimes do (and those are, no doubt, my worst moments) but that is not why I love myself. In fact it is the other way round: my self-love makes me think myself nice, but thinking myself nice is not why I love myself. So loving my enemies does not apparently mean thinking them nice either. That is an enormous relief. For a good many people imagine that forgiving your enemies means making out that they are really not such bad fellows after all, when it is quite plain that they are. Go a step further. In my most clear-sighted moments not only do I not think myself a nice man, but I know that I am a very nasty one. I can look at some of the things I have done with horror and loathing. So apparently I am allowed to loathe and hate some of the things my enemies do. Now that I come to think of it, I remember Christian teachers telling me long ago that I must hate a bad man's actions, but not hate the bad man: or, as they would say, hate the sin but not the sinner.

For a long time I used to think this a silly, straw-splitting distinction: how could you hate what a man did and not hate the man? But years later it occurred to me that there was one man to whom I had been doing this all my life—namely myself. However much I might dislike my own cowardice or conceit or greed, I went on loving myself. There had never been the slightest difficulty about it. In fact the very reason why I hated the things was that I loved the man. Just because I loved myself, I was sorry to find that I was the sort of man who did those things. Consequently, Christianity does not want us to reduce by one atom the hatred we feel for cruelty and treachery. We ought to hate them. Not one word of what we have said about them needs to be unsaid. But it does want us to hate them in the same way in which we hate things in ourselves: being sorry that the man should have done such things, and hoping, if it is anyway possible, that somehow, sometime, somewhere, he can be cured and made human again.

The real test is this. Suppose one reads a story of filthy atrocities in the paper. Then suppose that something turns up suggesting that the story might not be quite true, or not quite so bad as it was made out. Is one's first feeling, "Thank God, even they aren't quite so bad as that," or is it a feeling of disappointment, and even a determination to cling to the first story for the sheer pleasure of thinking your enemies as bad as possible? If it is the second then it is, I am afraid, the first step in a process which, if followed to the end, will make us into devils. You see, one is beginning to wish that black was a little blacker. If we give that wish its head, later on we shall wish to see grey as black, and then to see white itself as black. Finally, we shall insist on seeing everything—God and our friends and ourselves included—as bad, and not be able to stop doing it: we shall be fixed for ever in a universe of pure hatred.

Now a step further. Does loving your enemy mean not punishing him? No, for loving myself does not mean that I ought not to subject myself to punishment—even to death. If one had committed a murder, the right Christian thing to do would be to give yourself up to the police and be hanged. It is, therefore, in my opinion, perfectly right for a Christian judge to sentence a man to death or a Christian soldier to kill an enemy. I always have thought so, ever since I became a Christian, and long before the war, and I still think so now that we are at peace. It is no good quoting "Thou shalt not kill." There are two Greek words: the ordinary word to *kill* and the word to *murder*. And when Christ quotes that commandment He uses the *murder* one in all three accounts, Matthew, Mark, and Luke. And I am told there is the same distinction in Hebrew. All killing is not murder any more than all sexual intercourse is adultery. When soldiers came to St. John the Baptist asking what to do, he never remotely suggested that they ought to leave the army: nor did Christ when He met a Roman sergeant-major—what they called a centurion. The idea of the knight—the Christian in arms for the defence of a good cause—is one of the great Christian ideas. War is a dreadful thing, and I can respect an honest pacifist, though I think he is entirely mistaken. What I cannot understand is this sort of semipacifism you get nowadays which gives people the idea that though you have to fight, you ought to do it with a long face and as if you were ashamed of it. It is that feeling that robs lots of magnificent young Christians in the Services of something they have a right to, something which is the natural accompaniment of courage—a kind of gaiety and wholeheartedness.

I have often thought to myself how it would have been if, when I served in the first world war, I and some young German had killed each other simultaneously and found ourselves together a moment after death. I cannot imagine that either of us would have felt any resentment or even any embarrassment. I think we might have laughed over it.

I imagine somebody will say, "Well, if one is allowed to condemn the enemy's acts, and punish him, and kill him, what difference is left between Christian morality and the ordinary view?" All the difference in the world. Remember, we Christians think man lives for ever. Therefore, what really matters is those little marks or twists on the central, inside part of the soul which are going to turn it, in the long run, into a heavenly or a hellish creature. We may kill if necessary, but we must not hate and enjoy hating. We may punish if necessary, but we must not enjoy it. In other words, something inside us, the feeling of resentment, the feeling that wants to get one's own back, must be simply killed. I do not mean that anyone can decide this moment that he will never feel it any more. That is not how things happen. I mean that every time it bobs its head up, day after day, year after year, all our lives long, we must hit it on the head. It is hard work, but the attempt is not impossible. Even while we kill and punish we must try to feel about the enemy as we feel about ourselves—to wish that he were not bad, to hope that he may, in this world or another, be cured: in fact, to wish his good. That is what is meant in the Bible by loving him: wishing his good, not feeling fond of him nor saying he is nice when he is not.

I admit that this means loving people who have nothing lovable about them. But then, has oneself anything lovable about it? You love it simply because it is yourself. God intends us to love all selves in the same way and for the same reason: but He has given us the sum ready worked out on our own case to show us how it works. We have then to go on and apply the rule to all the other selves. Perhaps it makes it easier if we remember that that is how He loves us. Not for any nice, attractive qualities we think we have, but just because we are the things called selves. For really there is nothing else in us to love: creatures like us who actually find hatred such a pleasure that to give it up is like giving up beer or tobacco. . . .

CHAPTER 8
The Great Sin

❋

TODAY I COME to that part of Christian morals where they differ most sharply from all other morals. There is one vice of which no man in the world is free; which every one in the world loathes when he sees it in someone else; and of which hardly any people, except Christians, ever imagine that they are guilty themselves. I have heard people admit that they are bad-tempered, or that they cannot keep their heads about girls or drink, or even that they are cowards. I do not think I have ever heard anyone who was not a Christian accuse himself of this vice. And at the same time I have very seldom met anyone, who was not a Christian, who showed the slightest mercy to it in others. There is no fault which makes a man more unpopular, and no fault which we are more unconscious of in ourselves. And the more we have it ourselves, the more we dislike it in others.

The vice I am talking of is Pride or Self-Conceit: and the virtue opposite to it, in Christian morals, is called Humility. You may remember, when I was talking about sexual morality, I warned you that the centre of Christian morals did not lie there. Well, now, we have come to the centre. According to Christian teachers, the essential vice, the utmost evil, is Pride. Unchastity, anger, greed, drunkenness, and all that, are mere fleabites in comparison: it was through Pride that the devil became the devil: Pride leads to every other vice: it is the complete anti-God state of mind.

Does this seem to you exaggerated? If so, think it over. I pointed out a moment ago that the more pride one had, the more one disliked pride in others. In fact, if you want to find out how proud you are the easiest way is to ask yourself, "How much do I dislike it when other people snub me, or refuse to take any notice of me, or shove their oar in, or patronise me, or show off?" The point is that each person's pride is in competition with every one else's pride. It is because I wanted to be the big noise at the party that I am so annoyed at someone else being the big noise. Two of a trade never agree. Now what you want to get clear is that Pride is *essentially* competitive—is competitive by its very nature—while the other vices are competitive only, so to speak, by accident. Pride gets no pleasure out of having something, only out of having more of it than the next man. We say that people are proud of being rich, or clever, or good-looking, but they are not. They are proud of being richer, or cleverer, or better-looking than others. If every one else became equally rich, or clever, or good-looking there would be nothing to be proud about. It is the comparison that makes you proud: the pleasure of being above the rest. Once the element of competition has gone, pride has gone. That is why I say that Pride is essentially competitive in a way the other vices are not. The sexual impulse may drive two men into competition if they both want the same girl. But that is only by accident; they might just as likely have wanted two different girls. But a proud man will take your girl from you, not because he wants her, but just to prove to himself that he is a better man than you. Greed may drive men into competition if there is not enough to go round; but the proud man, even when he has got more than he can possibly want, will try to get still more just to assert his power. Nearly all those evils in the world which people put down to greed or selfishness are really far more the result of Pride.

Take it with money. Greed will certainly make a man want money, for the sake of a better house, better holidays, better things to eat and drink. But only up to a point. What is it that makes a man with £10,000 a year anxious to get £20,000 a year? It is not the greed for more pleasure. £10,000 will give all the luxuries that any man can really enjoy. It is Pride—the wish to be richer than some other rich man, and (still more) the wish for power. For, of course, power is what Pride really enjoys: there is nothing makes a man feel so superior to others as being able to move them about like toy soldiers. What makes a pretty girl spread misery wherever she goes by collecting admirers? Certainly not her sexual instinct: that kind of girl is quite often sexually frigid. It is Pride. What is it that makes a political leader or a whole nation go on and on, demanding more and more? Pride again. Pride is competitive by its very nature: that is why it goes on and on. If I am a proud man, then, as long as there is one man in the whole world more powerful, or richer, or clever than I, he is my rival and my enemy.

The Christians are right: it is Pride which has been the chief cause of misery in every nation and every family since the world began. Other vices may sometimes bring people together: you may find good fellowship and jokes and friendliness among drunken people or unchaste people. But Pride always means enmity—it *is* enmity. And not only enmity between man and man, but enmity to God.

In God you come up against something which is in every respect immeasurably superior to yourself. Unless you know God as that—and, therefore, know yourself as nothing in comparison—you do not know God at all. As long as you are proud you cannot know God. A proud man is always looking down on things and people: and, of course, as long as you are looking down, you cannot see something that is above you.

That raises a terrible question. How is it that people who are quite obviously eaten up with Pride can say they believe in God and appear to themselves very religious? I am afraid it means they are worshipping an imaginary God. They theoretically admit themselves to be nothing in the presence of this phantom God, but are really all the time imagining how He approves of them and thinks them far better than ordinary people: that is, they pay a pennyworth of imaginary humility to Him and get out of it a pound's worth of Pride towards their fellow-men. I suppose it was of those people Christ was thinking when He said that some would preach about Him and cast out devils in His name, only to be told at the end of the world that He had never known them. And any of us may at any moment be in this death-trap. Luckily, we have a test. Whenever we find that our religious life is making us feel that we are good—above all, that we are better than someone else—I think we may be sure that we are being acted on, not by God, but by the devil. The real test of being in the presence of God is that you either forget about yourself altogether or see yourself as a small, dirty object. It is better to forget about yourself altogether.

It is a terrible thing that the worst of all the vices can smuggle itself into the very centre of our religious life. But you can see why. The other, and less bad, vices come from the devil working on us through our animal nature. But this does not come through our animal nature at all. It comes direct from Hell. It is purely spiritual: consequently it is far more subtle and deadly. For the same reason, Pride can often be used to beat down the simpler vices. Teachers, in fact, often appeal to a boy's Pride, or, as they call it, his self-respect, to make him behave decently: many a man has overcome cowardice, or lust, or ill-temper by learning to think that they are beneath his dignity—that is, by Pride. The devil laughs. He is perfectly content to see you becoming chaste and brave and self-controlled provided, all the time, he is setting up in you the Dictatorship of Pride—just as he would be quite content to see your chilblains cured if he was allowed, in return, to give you cancer. For Pride is spiritual cancer: it eats up the very possibility of love, or contentment, or even common sense.

Before leaving this subject I must guard against some possible misunderstandings:

(1) Pleasure in being praised is not Pride. The child who is patted on the back for doing a lesson well, the woman whose beauty is praised by her lover, the saved soul to whom Christ says "Well done," are pleased and ought to be. For here the pleasure lies not in what you are but in the fact that you have pleased someone you wanted (and rightly wanted) to please. The trouble begins when you pass from thinking, "I have pleased him; all is well," to thinking, "What a fine person I must be to have done it." The more you delight in yourself and the less you delight in the praise, the worse you are becoming. When you delight wholly in yourself and do not care about the praise at all, you have reached the bottom. That is why vanity, though it is the sort of Pride which shows most on the surface, is really the least bad and most pardonable sort. The vain person wants praise, applause, admiration, too much and is always angling for it. It is a fault, but a childlike and even (in an odd way) a humble fault. It shows that you are not yet completely contented with your own admiration. You value other people enough to want them to look at you. You are, in fact, still human. The real black, diabolical Pride comes when you look down on others so much that you do not care what they think of you. Of course, it is very right, and often our duty, not to care what people think of us, if we do so for the right reason; namely, because we care so incomparably more what God thinks. But the Proud man has a different reason for not caring. He says "Why should I care for the applause of that rabble as if their opinion were worth anything? And even if their opinions were of value, am I the sort of man to blush with pleasure at a compliment like some chit of a girl at her first dance? No, I am an integrated, adult personality. All I have done has been done to satisfy my own ideals—or my artistic conscience—or the traditions of my family—or, in a word, because I'm That Kind of Chap. If the mob like it, let them. They're nothing to me." In this way real

thoroughgoing Pride may act as a check on vanity; for, as I said a moment ago, the devil loves "curing" a small fault by giving you a great one. We must try not to be vain, but we must never call in our Pride to cure our vanity; better the frying-pan than the fire.

(2) We say in English that a man is "proud" of his son, or his father, or his school, or regiment, and it may be asked whether "pride" in this sense is a sin. I think it depends on what, exactly, we mean by "proud of." Very often, in such sentences, the phrase "is proud of" means "has a warm-hearted admiration for." Such an admiration is, of course, very far from being a sin. But it might, perhaps, mean that the person in question gives himself airs on the ground of his distinguished father, or because he belongs to a famous regiment. This would, clearly, be a fault; but even then, it would be better than being proud simply of himself. To love and admire anything outside yourself is to take one step away from utter spiritual ruin; though we shall not be well so long as we love and admire anything more than we love and admire God.

(3) We must not think Pride is something God forbids because He is offended at it, or that Humility is something He demands as due to His own dignity—as if God Himself was proud. He is not in the least worried about His dignity. The point is, He wants you to know Him; wants to give you Himself. And He and you are two things of such a kind that if you really get into any kind of touch with Him you will, in fact, be humble—delightedly humble, feeling the infinite relief of having for once got rid of all the silly nonsense about your own dignity which has made you restless and unhappy all your life. He is trying to make you humble in order to make this moment possible: trying to take off a lot of silly, ugly, fancy-dress in which we have all got ourselves up and are strutting about like the little idiots we are. I wish I had got a bit further with humility myself: if I had, I could probably tell you more about the relief, the comfort, of taking the fancy-dress off— getting rid of the false self, with all its "Look at me" and

"Aren't I a good boy?" and all its posing and posturing. To get even near it, even for a moment, is like a drink of cold water to a man in a desert.

(4) Do not imagine that if you meet a really humble man he will be what most people call "humble" nowadays: he will not be a sort of greasy, smarmy person, who is always telling you that, of course, he is nobody. Probably all you will think about him is that he seemed a cheerful, intelligent chap who took a real interest in what *you* said to *him*. If you do dislike him it will be because you feel a little envious of anyone who seems to enjoy life so easily. He will not be thinking about humility: he will not be thinking about himself at all.

If anyone would like to acquire humility, I can, I think, tell him the first step. The first step is to realise that one is proud. And a biggish step, too. At least, nothing whatever can be done before it. If you think you are not conceited, it means you are very conceited indeed.

CHAPTER 9

Charity

✦

I SAID IN AN EARLIER CHAPTER that there were four "Cardinal" virtues and three "Theological" virtues. The three Theological ones are Faith, Hope, and Charity. Faith is going to be dealt with in the last two chapters. Charity was partly dealt with in Chapter 7, but there I concentrated on that part of Charity which is called Forgiveness. I now want to add a little more.

First, as to the meaning of the word. "Charity" now means simply what used to be called "alms"—that is, giving to the poor. Originally it had a much wider meaning. (You can see how it got the modern sense. If a man has "charity," giving to the poor is one of the most obvious things he does, and so people came to talk as if that were the whole of charity. In the same way, "rhyme" is the most obvious thing about poetry, and so people come to mean by "poetry" simply rhyme and nothing more.) Charity means "Love, in the Christian sense." But love, in the Christian sense, does not mean an emotion. It is a state not of the feelings but of the will; that state of the will which we have naturally about ourselves, and must learn to have about other people.

I pointed out in the chapter on Forgiveness that our love for ourselves does not mean that we *like* ourselves. It means that we wish our own good. In the same way Christian Love (or

Charity) for our neighbours is quite a different thing from liking or affection. We "like" or are "fond of" some people, and not of others. It is important to understand that this natural "liking" is neither a sin nor a virtue, any more than your likes and dislikes in food are a sin or a virtue. It is just a fact. But, of course, what we do about it is either sinful or virtuous.

Natural liking or affection for people makes it easier to be "charitable" towards them. It is, therefore, normally a duty to encourage our affections—to "like" people as much as we can (just as it is often our duty to encourage our liking for exercise or wholesome food)—not because this liking is itself the virtue of charity, but because it is a help to it. On the other hand, it is also necessary to keep a very sharp look-out for fear our liking for some one person makes us uncharitable, or even unfair, to someone else. There are even cases where our liking conflicts with our charity towards the person we like. For example, a doting mother may be tempted by natural affection to "spoil" her child; that is, to gratify her own affectionate impulses at the expense of the child's real happiness later on.

But though natural likings should normally be encouraged, it would be quite wrong to think that the way to become charitable is to sit trying to manufacture affectionate feelings. Some people are "cold" by temperament; that may be a misfortune for them, but it is no more a sin than having a bad digestion is a sin; and it does not cut them out from the chance, or excuse them from the duty, of learning charity. The rule for all of us is perfectly simple. Do not waste time bothering whether you "love" your neighbour; act as if you did. As soon as we do this we find one of the great secrets. When you are behaving as if you loved someone, you will presently come to love him. If you injure someone you dislike, you will find yourself disliking him more. If you do him a good turn, you will find yourself disliking him less. There is, indeed, one exception. If you do him a good turn, not to please God and obey the law of charity, but to show him what a fine forgiving chap you are, and to put him in your debt, and then sit down to wait for his "gratitude," you will probably be disappointed. (People are not fools: they have a very quick eye for anything like showing off, or patronage.) But whenever we do good to another self, just because it is a self, made (like us) by God, and desiring its own happiness as we desire ours, we shall have learned to love it a little more or, at least, to dislike it less.

Consequently, though Christian charity sounds a very cold thing to people whose heads are full of sentimentality, and though it is quite distinct from affection, yet it leads to affection. The difference between a Christian and a worldly man is not that the worldly man has only affections or "likings" and the Christian has only "charity." The worldly man treats certain people kindly because he "likes" them: the Christian, trying to treat every one kindly, finds himself liking more and more people as he goes on—including people he could not even have imagined himself liking at the beginning.

This same spiritual law works terribly in the opposite direction. The Germans, perhaps, at first ill-treated the Jews because they hated them: afterwards they hated them much more because they had ill-treated them. The more cruel you are, the more you will hate; and the more you hate, the more cruel you will become—and so on in a vicious circle for ever.

Good and evil both increase at compound interest. That is why the little decisions you and I make every day are of such infinite importance. The smallest good act today is the capture of a strategic point from which, a few months later, you may be able to go on to victories you never dreamed of. An apparently trivial indulgence in lust or anger today is the loss of a ridge or railway line or bridgehead from which the enemy may launch an attack otherwise impossible.

Some writers use the word charity to describe not only Christian love between human beings, but also God's love for man and man's love for God. About the second of these two, people are often worried. They are told they ought to love God. They cannot find any such feeling in themselves. What are they to do? The answer is the same as before. Act as if you did. Do not sit trying to manufacture feelings. Ask yourself, "If I were sure that I loved God, what would I do?" When you have found the answer, go and do it.

On the whole, God's love for us is a much safer subject to think about than our love for Him. Nobody can always have devout feelings: and even if we could, feelings are not what God principally cares about. Christian Love, either towards God or towards man, is an affair of the will. If we are trying to do His will we are obeying the commandment, "Thou shalt love the Lord thy God." He will give us feelings of love if He pleases. We cannot create them for ourselves, and we must not demand them as a right. But the great thing to remember is that, though our feelings come and go, His love for us does not. It is not wearied by our sins, or our indifference; and, therefore, it is quite relentless in its determination that we shall be cured of those sins, at whatever cost to us, at whatever cost to Him.

CHAPTER 10

Hope

❋

Hope is one of the Theological virtues. This means that a continual looking forward to the eternal world is not (as some modern people think) a form of escapism or wishful thinking, but one of the things a Christian is meant to do. It does not mean that we are to leave the present world as it is. If you read history you will find that the Christians who did most for the present world were just those who thought most of the next. The Apostles themselves, who set on foot the conversion of the Roman Empire, the great men who built up the Middle Ages, the English Evangelicals who abolished the Slave Trade, all left their mark on Earth, precisely because their minds were occupied with Heaven. It is since Christians have largely ceased to think of the other world that they have become so ineffective in this. Aim at Heaven and you will get earth "thrown in": aim at earth and you will get neither. It seems a strange rule, but something like it can be seen at work in other matters. Health is a great blessing, but the moment you make health one of your main, direct objects you start becoming a crank and imagining there is something wrong with you. You are only likely to get health provided you want other things more—food, games, work, fun, open air. In the same way, we shall never save civilisation as long as civilisation is our main object. We must learn to want something else even more.

Most of us find it very difficult to want "Heaven" at all—except in so far as "Heaven" means meeting again our friends who have died. One reason for this difficulty is that we have not been trained: our whole education tends to fix our minds on this world. Another reason is that when the real want for Heaven is present in us, we do not recognise it. Most people, if they had really learned to look into their own hearts, would know that they do want, and want acutely, something that cannot be had in this world. There are all sorts of things in this world that offer to give it to you, but they never quite keep their promise. The longings which arise in us when we first fall in love, or first think of some foreign country, or first take up some subject that excites us, are longings which no marriage, no travel, no learning, can really satisfy. I am not now speaking of what would be ordinarily called unsuccessful marriages, or holidays, or learned careers. I am speaking of the best possible ones. There was something we grasped at, in that first moment of longing, which just fades away in the reality. I think everyone knows what I mean. The wife may be a good wife, and the hotels and scenery may have been excellent, and chemistry may be a very interesting job: but something has evaded us. Now there are two wrong ways of dealing with this fact, and one right one.

(1) The Fool's Way.—He puts the blame on the things themselves. He goes on all his life thinking that if only he tried another woman, or went for a more expensive holiday, or whatever it is, then, this time, he really would catch the mysterious something we are all after. Most of the bored, discontented, rich people in the world are of this type. They spend their whole lives trotting from woman to woman (through the divorce courts), from continent to continent, from hobby to hobby, always thinking that the latest is "the Real Thing" at last, and always disappointed.

(2) The Way of the Disillusioned "Sensible Man."—He soon decides that the whole thing was moonshine. "Of course," he says, "one feels like that when one's young. But by the time

you get to my age you've given up chasing the rainbow's end." And so he settles down and learns not to expect too much and represses the part of himself which used, as he would say, "to cry for the moon." This is, of course, a much better way than the first, and makes a man much happier, and less of a nuisance to society. It tends to make him a prig (he is apt to be rather superior towards what he calls "adolescents"), but, on the whole, he rubs along fairly comfortably. It would be the best line we could take if man did not live for ever. But supposing infinite happiness really is there, waiting for us? Supposing one really can reach the rainbow's end? In that case it would be a pity to find out too late (a moment after death) that by our supposed "common sense" we had stifled in ourselves the faculty of enjoying it.

(3) The Christian Way.—The Christian says, "Creatures are not born with desires unless satisfaction for those desires exists. A baby feels hunger: well, there is such a thing as food. A duckling wants to swim: well, there is such a thing as water. Men feel sexual desire: well, there is such a thing as sex. If I find in myself a desire which no experience in this world can satisfy, the most probable explanation is that I was made for another world. If none of my earthly pleasures satisfy it, that does not prove that the universe is a fraud. Probably earthly pleasures were never meant to satisfy it, but only to arouse it, to suggest the real thing. If that is so, I must take care, on the one hand, never to despise, or be unthankful for, these earthly blessings, and on the other, never to mistake them for the something else of which they are only a kind of copy, or echo, or mirage. I must keep alive in myself the desire for my true country, which I shall not find till after death; I must never let it get snowed under or turned aside; I must make it the main object of life to press on to that other country and to help others to do the same."

There is no need to be worried by facetious people who try to make the Christian hope of "Heaven" ridiculous by saying they do not want "to spend eternity playing harps." The answer to such people is that if they cannot understand books written for grown-ups, they should not talk about them. All the scriptural imagery (harps, crowns, gold, etc.) is, of course, a merely symbolical attempt to express the inexpressible. Musical instruments are mentioned because for many people (not all) music is the thing known in the present life which most strongly suggests ecstasy and infinity. Crowns are mentioned to suggest the fact that those who are united with God in eternity share His splendour and power and joy. Gold is mentioned to suggest the timelessness of Heaven (gold does not rust) and the preciousness of it. People who take these symbols literally might as well think that when Christ told us to be like doves, He meant that we were to lay eggs.

CHAPTER 11
Faith

I MUST TALK IN THIS CHAPTER about what the Christians call Faith. Roughly speaking, the word Faith seems to be used by Christians in two senses or on two levels, and I will take them in turn. In the first sense it means simply Belief—accepting or regarding as true the doctrines of Christianity. That is fairly simple. But what does puzzle people—at least it used to puzzle me—is the fact that Christians regard faith in this sense as a virtue. I used to ask how on earth it can be a virtue—what is there moral or immoral about believing or not believing a set of statements? Obviously, I used to say, a sane man accepts or rejects any statement, not because he wants or does not want to, but because the evidence seems to him good or bad. If he were mistaken about the goodness or badness of the evidence that would not mean he was a bad man, but only that he was not very clever. And if he thought the evidence bad but tried to force himself to believe in spite of it, that would be merely stupid.

Well, I think I still take that view. But what I did not see then—and a good many people do not see still—was this. I was assuming that if the human mind once accepts a thing as true it will automatically go on regarding it as true, until some real reason for reconsidering it turns up. In fact, I was assuming that the human mind is completely ruled by reason. But that is not so. For example, my reason is perfectly convinced by good evidence that anaesthetics do not smother me and that properly trained surgeons do not start operating until I am unconscious. But the idea does not alter the fact that when they have me down on the table and clap their horrible mask over my face, a mere childish panic begins inside me. I start thinking I am going to choke, and I am afraid they will start cutting me up before I am properly under. In other words, I lose my faith in anaesthetics. It is not reason that is taking away my faith: on the contrary, my faith is based on reason. It is my imagination and emotions. The battle is between faith and reason on one side and emotion and imagination on the other.

When you think of it you will see lots of instances of this. A man knows, on perfectly good evidence, that a pretty girl of his acquaintance is a liar and cannot keep a secret and ought not to be trusted; but when he finds himself with her his mind loses its faith in that bit of knowledge and he starts thinking, "Perhaps she'll be different this time," and once more makes a fool of himself and tells her something he ought not to have told her. His senses and emotions have destroyed his faith in what he really knows to be true. Or take a boy learning to swim. His reason knows perfectly well that an unsupported human body will not necessarily sink in water: he has seen dozens of people float and swim. But the whole question is whether he will be able to go on believing this when the instructor takes away his hand and leaves him unsupported in the water—or whether he will suddenly cease to believe it and get in a fright and go down.

Now just the same thing happens about Christianity. I am not asking anyone to accept Christianity if his best reasoning tells him that the weight of the evidence is against it. That is not the point at which Faith comes in. But supposing a man's reason once decides that the weight of the evidence is for it. I can tell that man what is going to happen to him in the next few weeks. There will come a moment when there is bad news, or he is in trouble, or is living among a lot of other people who do not believe it, and all at once his emotions will rise up and carry out a sort of blitz on his belief. Or else there will come a moment when he wants a woman, or wants to tell a lie, or feels very pleased with himself, or sees a chance of making a little money in some way that is not perfectly fair: some moment, in fact, at which it would be very convenient if Christianity were not true. And once again his wishes and desires will carry out a blitz. I am not talking of moments at which any real new reasons against Christianity turn up. Those have to be faced and that is a different matter. I am talking about moments where a mere mood rises up against it.

Now Faith, in the sense in which I am here using the word, is the art of holding on to things your reason has once accepted, in spite of your changing moods. For moods will change, whatever view your reason takes. I know that by experience. Now that I am a Christian I do have moods in which the whole thing looks very improbable: but when I was an atheist I had moods in which Christianity looked terribly probable. This rebellion of your moods against your real self is going to come anyway. That is why Faith is such a necessary virtue: unless you teach your moods "where they get off," you can never be either a sound Christian or even a sound atheist, but just a creature dithering to and fro, with its beliefs really dependent on the weather and the state of its digestion. Consequently one must train the habit of Faith.

The first step is to recognise the fact that your moods change. The next is to make sure that, if you have once accepted Christianity, then some of its main doctrines shall be deliberately held before your mind for some time every day. That is why daily prayers and religious reading and church-going are necessary parts of the Christian life. We have to be continually reminded of what we believe. Neither this belief nor any other will automatically remain alive in the mind. It must be fed. And as a matter of fact, if you examined a hundred people who had lost their faith in Christianity, I wonder how many of them would turn out to have been reasoned out of it by honest argument? Do not most people simply drift away?

Now I must turn to Faith in the second or higher sense: and this is the most difficult thing I have tackled yet. I want to approach it by going back to the subject of Humility. You may remember I said that the first step towards humility was to realise that one is proud. I want to add now that the next step is to make some serious attempt to practise the Christian virtues. A week is not enough. Things often go swimmingly for the first week. Try six weeks. By that time, having, as far as one can see, fallen back completely or even fallen lower than the point one began from, one will have discovered some truths about oneself. No man knows how bad he is till he has tried very hard to be good. A silly idea is current that good people do not know what temptation means. This is an obvious lie. Only those who try to resist temptation know how strong it is. After all, you find out the strength of the German army by fighting against it, not by giving in. You find out the strength of a wind by trying to walk against it, not by lying down. A man who gives in to temptation after five minutes simply does not know what it would have been like an hour later. That is why bad people, in one sense, know very little about badness. They have lived a sheltered life by always giving in. We never find out the strength of the evil impulse inside us until we try to fight it: and Christ, because He was the only man who never yielded to temptation, is also the only man who knows to the full what temptation means—the only complete realist. Very well, then. The main thing we learn from a serious attempt to practise the Christian virtues is that we fail. If there was any idea that God had set us a sort of exam. and that we might get good marks by deserving them, that has to be wiped out. If there was any idea of a sort of bargain—any idea that we could perform our side of the contract and thus put God in our debts so that it was up to Him, in mere justice, to perform His side—that has to be wiped out.

I think every one who has some vague belief in God, until he becomes a Christian, has the idea of an exam. or of a bargain in his mind. The first result of real Christianity is to blow that idea into bits. When they find it blown into bits, some people think this means that Christianity is a failure and give up. They seem to imagine that God is very simple-minded! In fact, of course, He knows all about this. One of the very things Christianity was designed to do was to blow this idea to bits. God has been waiting for the moment at which you discover that there is no question of earning a pass mark in this exam. or putting Him in your debt.

Then comes another discovery. Every faculty you have, your power of thinking or of moving your limbs from moment to moment, is given you by God. If you devoted every moment of your life exclusively to His service you could not give Him anything that was not in a sense His own already. So that when we talk of a man doing anything for God or giving anything to God, I will tell you what it is really like. It is like a small child going to its father and saying, "Daddy, give me sixpence to buy you a birthday present." Of course, the father does, and he is pleased with the child's present. It is all very nice and proper, but only an idiot would think that the father is sixpence to the good on the transaction. When a man has made these two discoveries God can really get to work. It is after this that real life begins. The man is awake now. We can now go on to talk of Faith in the second sense.

CHAPTER 12
Faith

***

I WANT TO START BY SAYING something that I would like everyone to notice carefully. It is this. If this chapter means nothing to you, if it seems to be trying to answer questions you never asked, drop it at once. Do not bother about it at all. There are certain things in Christianity that can be understood from the outside, before you have become a Christian. But there are a great many things that cannot be understood until after you have gone a certain distance along the Christian road. These things are purely practical, though they do not look as if they were. They are directions for dealing with particular cross-roads and obstacles on the journey and they do not make sense until a man has reached those places. Whenever you find any statement in Christian writings which you can make nothing of, do not worry. Leave it alone. There will come a day, perhaps years later, when you suddenly see what it meant. If one could understand it now, it would only do one harm.

Of course all this tells against me as much as anyone else. The thing I am going to try to explain in this chapter may be ahead of me. I may be thinking I have got there when I have not. I can only ask instructed Christians to watch very carefully, and tell me when I go wrong; and others to take what I say with a grain of salt—as something offered, because it may be a help, not because I am certain that I am right.

I am trying to talk about Faith in the second sense, the higher sense. I said last week that the question of Faith in this sense arises after a man has tried his level best to practise the Christian virtues, and found that he fails, and seen that even if he could he would only be giving back to God what was already God's own. In other words, he discovers his bankruptcy. Now, once again, what God cares about is not exactly our actions. What he cares about is that we should be creatures of a certain kind or quality—the kind of creatures He intended us to be—creatures related to Himself in a certain way. I do not add "and related to one another in a certain way," because that is included: if you are right with Him you will inevitably be right with all your fellow-creatures, just as if all the spokes of a wheel are fitted rightly into the hub and the rim they are bound to be in the right positions to one another. And as long as a man is thinking of God as an examiner who has set him a sort of paper to do, or as the opposite party in a sort of bargain—as long as he is thinking of claims and counterclaims between himself and God—he is not yet in the right relation to Him. He is misunderstanding what he is and what God is. And he cannot get into the right relation until he has discovered the fact of our bankruptcy.

When I say "discovered," I mean really discovered: not simply said it parrot-fashion. Of course, any child, if given a certain kind of religious education, will soon learn to *say* that we have nothing to offer to God that is not already His own and that we find ourselves failing to offer even that without keeping something back. But I am talking of really discovering this: really finding out by experience that it is true.

Now we cannot, in that sense, discover our failure to keep God's law except by trying our very hardest (and then failing). Unless we really try, whatever we say there will always be at the back of our minds the idea that if we try harder next time we shall succeed in being completely good. Thus, in one sense, the road back to God is a road of moral effort, of trying harder and harder. But in another sense it is not trying that is ever going to bring us home. All this trying leads up to the vital moment at which you turn to God and say, "You must do this. I can't." Do not, I implore you, start asking your-selves, "Have I reached that moment?" Do not sit down and start watching your own mind to see if it is coming along. That puts a man quite on the wrong track. When the most important things in our life happen we quite often do not know, at the moment, what is going on. A man does not al-ways say to himself, "Hullo! I'm growing up." It is often only when he looks back that he realises what has happened and recognises it as what people call "growing up." You can see it even in simple matters. A man who starts anxiously watching to see whether he is going to sleep is very likely to remain wide awake. As well, the thing I am talking of now may not happen to every one in a sudden flash—as it did to St. Paul or Bunyan: it may be so gradual that no one could ever point to a particular hour or even a particular year. And what matters is the nature of the change in itself, not how we feel while it is happening. It is the change from being confident about our own efforts to the state in which we despair of doing anything for ourselves and leave it to God.

I know the words "leave it to God" can be misunderstood, but they must stay for the moment. The sense in which a Christian leaves it to God is that he puts all his trust in Christ: trusts that Christ will somehow share with him the perfect hu-man obedience which He carried out from His birth to His crucifixion: that Christ will make the man more like Himself and, in a sense, make good his deficiencies. In Christian lan-guage, He will share His "sonship" with us, will make us, like Himself, "Sons of God": in Book IV I shall attempt to analyse the meaning of those words a little further. If you like to put it that way, Christ offers something for nothing: He even of-fers everything for nothing. In a sense, the whole Christian life consists in accepting that very remarkable offer. But the difficulty is to reach the point of recognising that all we have done and can do is nothing. What we should have liked would be for God to count our good points and ignore our bad ones. Again, in a sense, you may say that no temptation is ever overcome until we stop trying to overcome it—throw up the sponge. But then you could not "stop trying" in the right way and for the right reason until you had tried your very hardest. And, in yet another sense, handing everything over to Christ does not, of course, mean that you stop trying. To trust Him means, of course, trying to do all that He says. There would be no sense in saying you trusted a person if you would not take his advice. Thus if you have really handed yourself over to Him, it must follow that you are trying to obey Him. But trying in a new way, a less worried way. Not doing these things in order to be saved, but because He has begun to save you already. Not hoping to get to Heaven as a reward for your actions, but inevitably wanting to act in a certain way because a first faint gleam of Heaven is already inside you.

Christians have often disputed as to whether what leads the Christian home is good actions, or Faith in Christ. I have no right really to speak on such a difficult question, but it does seem to me like asking which blade in a pair of scissors is most necessary. A serious moral effort is the only thing that will bring you to the point where you throw up the sponge. Faith in Christ is the only thing to save you from despair at that point: and out of that Faith in Him good actions must inevitably come. There are two parodies of the truth which different sets of Christians have, in the past, been accused by other Christians of believing: perhaps they may make the truth clearer. One set were accused of saying, "Good actions are all that matters. The best good action is charity. The best kind of charity is giving money. The best thing to give money to is the Church. So hand us over £10,000 and we will see you through." The answer to that nonsense, of course, would be that good actions done for that motive, done with the idea that Heaven can be bought, would not be good actions at all, but only commercial speculations. The other set were accused of saying, "Faith is all that matters. Consequently, if you have faith, it doesn't matter what you do. Sin away, my lad, and have a good time and Christ will see that it makes no difference in the end." The answer to that nonsense is that, if what you call your "faith" in Christ does not involve taking the slightest notice of what He says, then it is not Faith at all—not faith or trust in Him, but only intellectual acceptance of some theory about Him.

The Bible really seems to clinch the matter when it puts the two things together into one amazing sentence. The first half is, "Work out your own salvation with fear and trembling"—which looks as if everything depended on us and our good actions: but the second half goes on, "For it is God who worketh in you"—which looks as if God did everything and we nothing. I am afraid that is the sort of thing we come up against in Christianity. I am puzzled, but I am not surprised. You see, we are now trying to understand, and to separate into water-tight compartments, what exactly God does and what man does when God and man are working together. And, of course, we begin by thinking it is like two men working together, so that you could say, "He did this bit and I did that." But this way of thinking breaks down. God is not like that. He is inside you as well as outside: even if we could understand who did what, I do not think human language could properly express it. In the attempt to express it different Churches say different things. But you will find that even those who insist most strongly on the importance of good actions tell you you need Faith; and even those who insist most strongly on Faith tell you to do good actions. At any rate that is as far as I go.

I think all Christians would agree with me if I said that though Christianity seems at first to be all about morality, all about duties and rules and guilt and virtue, yet it leads you on, out of all that, into something beyond. One has a glimpse of a country where they do not talk of those things, except perhaps as a joke. Every one there is filled full with what we should call goodness as a mirror is filled with light. But they do not call it goodness. They do not call it anything. They are not thinking of it. They are too busy looking at the source from which it comes. But this is near the stage where the road passes over the rim of our world. No one's eyes can see very far beyond that: lots of people's eyes can see further than mine.

BOOK IV

Beyond Personality: or First Steps in the Doctrine of the Trinity

CHAPTER 1
Making and Begetting

Everyone has warned me not to tell you what I am going to tell you in this last book. They all say "the ordinary reader does not want Theology; give him plain practical religion." I have rejected their advice. I do not think the ordinary reader is such a fool. Theology means "the science of God," and I think any man who wants to think about God at all would like to have the clearest and most accurate ideas about Him which are available. You are not children: why should you be treated like children?

In a way I quite understand why some people are put off by Theology. I remember once when I had been giving a talk to the R.A.F., an old, hard-bitten officer got up and said, "I've no use for all that stuff. But, mind you, I'm a religious man too. I *know* there's a God. I've *felt* Him: out alone in the desert at night: the tremendous mystery. And that's just why I don't believe all your neat little dogmas and formulas about Him. To anyone who's met the real thing they all seem so petty and pedantic and unreal!"

Now in a sense I quite agreed with that man. I think he had probably had a real experience of God in the desert. And when he turned from that experience to the Christian creeds, I think he really was turning from something real to something less real. In the same way, if a man has once looked at the Atlantic from the beach, and then goes and looks at a map of the Atlantic, he also will be turning from something real to something less real: turning from real waves to a bit of coloured paper. But here comes the point. The map is admittedly only coloured paper, but there are two things you have to remember about it. In the first place, it is based on what hundreds and thousands of people have found out by sailing the real Atlantic. In that way it has behind it masses of experience just as real as the one you could have from the beach; only, while yours would be a single isolated glimpse, the map fits all those different experiences together. In the second place, if you want to go anywhere, the map is absolutely necessary. As long as you are content with walks on the beach, your own glimpses are far more fun than looking at a map. But the map is going to be more use than walks on the beach if you want to get to America.

Now, Theology is like the map. Merely learning and thinking about the Christian doctrines, if you stop there, is less real and less exciting than the sort of thing my friend got in the desert. Doctrines are not God: they are only a kind of map. But that map is based on the experience of hundreds of people who really were in touch with God—experiences compared with which any thrills or pious feelings you and I are likely to get on our own are very elementary and very confused. And secondly, if you want to get any further, you must use the map. You see, what happened to that man in the desert may have been real, and was certainly exciting, but nothing comes of it. It leads nowhere. There is nothing to do about it. In fact that is just why a vague religion—all about feeling God in nature, and so on—is so attractive. It is all thrills and no work like watching the waves from the beach. But you will not get to Newfoundland by studying the Atlantic that way, and you will not get eternal life by simply feeling the presence of God in flowers or music. Neither will you get anywhere by looking at maps without going to sea. Nor will you be very safe if you go to sea without a map.

In other words, Theology is practical: especially now. In the old days, when there was less education and discussion, perhaps it was possible to get on with a very few simple ideas about God. But it is not so now. Everyone reads, everyone hears things discussed. Consequently, if you do not listen to Theology, that will not mean that you have no ideas about God. It will mean that you have a lot of wrong ones—bad, muddled, out-of-date ideas. For a great many of the ideas about God which are trotted out as novelties today, are simply the ones which real Theologians tried centuries ago and rejected. To believe in the popular religion of modern England is retrogression—like believing the earth is flat.

For when you get down to it, is not the popular idea of Christianity simply this: that Jesus Christ was a great moral teacher and that if only we took his advice we might be able to establish a better social order and avoid another war? Now, mind you, that is quite true. But it tells you much less than the whole truth about Christianity and it has no practical importance at all.

It is quite true that if we took Christ's advice we should soon be living in a happier world. You need not even go as far as Christ. If we did all that Plato or Aristotle or Confucius told us, we should get on a great deal better than we do. And so what? We never have followed the advice of the great teachers. Why are we likely to begin now? Why are we more likely to follow Christ than any of the others? Because He is the best moral teacher? But that makes it even less likely that we shall follow Him. If we cannot take the elementary lessons, is it likely we are going to take the most advanced one? If Christianity only means one more bit of good advice, then Christianity is of no importance. There has been no lack of good advice for the last four thousand years. A bit more makes no difference.

But as soon as you look at any real Christian writings, you find that they are talking about something quite different from this popular religion. They say that Christ is the Son of God (whatever that means). They say that those who give Him their confidence can also become Sons of God (whatever that means). They say that His death saved us from our sins (whatever that means).

There is no good complaining that these statements are difficult. Christianity claims to be telling us about another world, about something behind the world we can touch and hear and see. You may think the claim false; but if it were true, what it tells us would be bound to be difficult—at least as difficult as modern Physics, and for the same reason.

Now the point in Christianity which gives us the greatest shock is the statement that by attaching ourselves to Christ, we can "become Sons of God." One asks "Aren't we Sons of God already? Surely the fatherhood of God is one of the main Christian ideas?" Well, in a certain sense, no doubt we are sons of God already. I mean, God has brought us into existence and loves us and looks after us, and in that way is like a father. But when the Bible talks of our "becoming" Sons of God, obviously it must mean something different. And that brings us up against the very centre of Theology.

One of the creeds says that Christ is the Son of God "begotten, not created"; and it adds "begotten by his Father before all worlds." Will you please get it quite clear that this has nothing to do with the fact that when Christ was born on earth as a man, that man was the son of a virgin? We are not now thinking about the Virgin Birth. We are thinking about something that happened before Nature was created at all, before time began. "Before all worlds" Christ is begotten, not created. What does it mean?

We don't use the words *begetting* or *begotten* much in modern English, but everyone still knows what they mean. To beget is to become the father of: to create is to make. And the difference is this. When you beget, you beget something of the same kind as yourself. A man begets human babies, a beaver begets little beavers and a bird begets eggs which turn into little birds. But when you make, you make something of a different kind from yourself. A bird makes a nest, a beaver builds a dam, a man makes a wireless set—or he may make something more like himself than a wireless set: say, a statue. If he is a clever enough carver he may make a statue which is very like a man indeed. But, of course, it is not a real man; it only looks like one. It cannot breathe or think. It is not alive.

Now that is the first thing to get clear. What God begets is God; just as what man begets is man. What God creates is not God; just as what man makes is not man. That is why men are not Sons of God in the sense that Christ is. They may be like God in certain ways, but they are not things of the same kind. They are more like statues or pictures of God.

A statue has the shape of a man but it is not alive. In the same way, man has (in a sense I am going to explain) the "shape" or likeness of God, but he has not got the kind of life God has. Let us take the first point (man's resemblance to God) first. Everything God has made has some likeness to Himself. Space is like Him in its hugeness: not that the greatness of space is the same kind of greatness as God's, but it is a sort of symbol of it, or a translation of it into non-spiritual terms. Matter is like God in having energy: though, again, of course, physical energy is a different kind of thing from the power of God. The vegetable world is like Him because it is alive, and He is the "living God." But life, in this biological sense, is not the same as the life there is in God: it is only a kind of symbol or shadow of it. When we come on to the animals, we find other kinds of resemblance in addition to biological life. The intense activity and fertility of the insects, for example, is a first dim resemblance to the unceasing activity and the creativeness of God. In the higher mammals we get the beginnings of instinctive affection. That is not the same thing as the love that exists in God: but it is like it—rather in the way that a picture drawn on a flat piece of paper can nevertheless be "like" a landscape. When we come to man, the highest of the animals, we get the completest resemblance to God which we know of. (There may be creatures in other worlds who are more like God than man is, but we do not know about them.) Man not only lives, but loves and reasons: biological life reaches its highest known level in him.

But what man, in his natural condition, has not got, is Spiritual life—the higher and different sort of life that exists in God. We use the same word *life* for both: but if you thought that both must therefore be the same sort of thing, that would be like thinking that the "greatness" of space and the "greatness" of God were the same sort of greatness. In reality, the difference between Biological life and Spiritual life is so important that I am going to give them two distinct names. The Biological sort which comes to us through Nature, and which (like everything else in Nature) is always tending to run down and decay so that it can only be kept up by incessant subsidies from Nature in the form of air, water, food, etc., is *Bios*. The Spiritual life which is in God from all eternity, and which made the whole natural universe, is *Zoe*. *Bios* has, to be sure, a certain shadowy or symbolic resemblance to *Zoe*: but only the sort of resemblance there is between a photo and a place, or a statue and a man. A man who changed from having *Bios* to having *Zoe* would have gone through as big a change as a statue which changed from being a carved stone to being a real man.

And that is precisely what Christianity is about. This world is a great sculptor's shop. We are the statues and there is a rumour going round the shop that some of us are some day going to come to life.

CHAPTER 2

The Three-Personal God

THE LAST CHAPTER was about the difference between begetting and making. A man begets a child, but he only makes a statue. God begets Christ but He only makes men. But by saying that, I have illustrated only one point about God, namely, that what God the Father begets is God, something of the same kind as Himself. In that way it is like a human father begetting a human son. But not quite like it. So I must try to explain a little more.

A good many people nowadays say, "I believe in a God, but not in a personal God." They feel that the mysterious something which is behind all other things must be more than a person. Now the Christians quite agree. But the Christians are the only people who offer any idea of what a being that is beyond personality could be like. All the other people, though they say that God is beyond personality, really think of Him as something impersonal: that is, as something less than personal. If you are looking for something super-personal, something more than a person, then it is not a question of choosing between the Christian idea and the other ideas. The Christian idea is the only one on the market.

Again, some people think that after this life, or perhaps after several lives, human souls will be "absorbed" into God. But

137

when they try to explain what they mean, they seem to be thinking of our being absorbed into God as one material thing is absorbed into another. They say it is like a drop of water slipping into the sea. But of course that is the end of the drop. If that is what happens to us, then being absorbed is the same as ceasing to exist. It is only the Christians who have any idea of how human souls can be taken into the life of God and yet remain themselves—in fact, be very much more themselves than they were before.

I warned you that Theology is practical. The whole purpose for which we exist is to be thus taken into the life of God. Wrong ideas about what that life is, will make it harder. And now, for a few minutes, I must ask you to follow rather carefully.

You know that in space you can move in three ways—to left or right, backwards or forwards, up or down. Every direction is either one of these three or a compromise between them. They are called the three Dimensions. Now notice this. If you are using only one dimension, you could draw only a straight line. If you are using two, you could draw a figure: say, a square. And a square is made up of four straight lines. Now a step further. If you have three dimensions, you can then build what we call a solid body, say, a cube—a thing like a dice or a lump of sugar. And a cube is made up of six squares.

Do you see the point? A world of one dimension would be a straight line. In a two-dimensional world, you still get straight lines, but many lines make one figure. In a three-dimensional world, you still get figures but many figures make one solid body. In other words, as you advance to more real and more complicated levels, you do not leave behind you the things you found on the simpler levels: you still have them, but combined in new ways—in ways you could not imagine if you knew only the simpler levels.

Now the Christian account of God involves just the same principle. The human level is a simple and rather empty level. On the human level one person is one being, and any two persons are two separate beings—just as, in two dimensions (say on a flat sheet of paper) one square is one figure, and any two squares are two separate figures. On the Divine level you still find personalities; but up there you find them combined in new ways which we, who do not live on that level, cannot imagine. In God's dimension, so to speak, you find a being who is three Persons while remaining one Being, just as a cube is six squares while remaining one cube. Of course we cannot fully conceive a Being like that: just as, if we were so made that we perceived only two dimensions in space we could never properly imagine a cube. But we can get a sort of faint notion of it. And when we do, we are then, for the first time in our lives, getting some positive idea, however faint, of something super-personal—something more than a person. It is something we could never have guessed, and yet, once we have been told, one almost feels one ought to have been able to guess it because it fits in so well with all the things we know already.

You may ask, "If we cannot imagine a three-personal Being, what is the good of talking about Him?" Well, there isn't any good talking about Him. The thing that matters is being actually drawn into that three-personal life, and that may begin any time—tonight, if you like.

What I mean is this. An ordinary simple Christian kneels down to say his prayers. He is trying to get into touch with God. But if he is a Christian he knows that what is prompting him to pray is also God: God, so to speak, inside him. But he also knows that all his real knowledge of God comes through Christ, the Man who was God—that Christ is standing beside him, helping him to pray, praying for him. You see what is happening. God is the thing to which he is praying—the goal he is trying to reach. God is also the thing inside him which is pushing him on—the motive power. God is also the road or bridge along which he is being pushed to that goal. So that the whole threefold life of the three-personal Being is actually going on in that ordinary little bedroom where an ordinary man is saying his prayers. The man is being caught up into the higher kind of life—what I called *Zoe* or spiritual life: he is being pulled into God, by God, while still remaining himself.

And that is how Theology started. People already knew about God in a vague way. Then came a man who claimed to be God; and yet he was not the sort of man you could dismiss as a lunatic. He made them believe Him. They met Him again after they had seen Him killed. And then, after they had been formed into a little society or community, they found God somehow inside them as well: directing them, making them able to do things they could not do before. And when they worked it all out they found they had arrived at the Christian definition of the three-personal God.

This definition is not something we have made up; Theology is, in a sense, experimental knowledge. It is the simple religions that are the made-up ones. When I say it is an experimental science "in a sense," I mean that it is like the other experimental sciences in some ways, but not in all. If you are a geologist studying rocks, you have to go and find the rocks. They will not come to you, and if you go to them they cannot run away. The initiative lies all on your side. They cannot either help or hinder. But suppose you are a zoologist and want to take photos of wild animals in their native haunts. That is a bit different from studying rocks. The wild animals will not come to you: but they can run away from you. Unless you keep very quiet, they will. There is beginning to be a tiny little trace of initiative on their side.

Now a stage higher; suppose you want to get to know a human person. If he is determined not to let you, you will not get to know him. You have to win his confidence. In this case the initiative is equally divided—it takes two to make a friendship.

When you come to knowing God, the initiative lies on His side. If He does not show Himself, nothing you can do will enable you to find Him. And, in fact, He shows much more of Himself to some people than to others—not because He has favourites, but because it is impossible for Him to show Himself to a man whose whole mind and character are in the wrong condition. Just as sunlight, though it has no favourites, cannot be reflected in a dusty mirror as clearly as in a clean one.

You can put this another way by saying that while in other sciences the instruments you use are things external to yourself (things like microscopes and telescopes), the instrument through which you see God is your whole self. And if a man's self is not kept clean and bright, his glimpse of God will be blurred—like the Moon seen through a dirty telescope. That is why horrible nations have horrible religions: they have been looking at God through a dirty lens.

God can show Himself as He really is only to real men. And that means not simply to men who are individually good, but to men who are united together in a body, loving one another, helping one another, showing Him to one another. For that is what God meant humanity to be like; like players in one band, or organs in one body.

Consequently, the one really adequate instrument for learning about God, is the whole Christian community, waiting for Him together. Christian brotherhood is, so to speak, the technical equipment for this science—the laboratory outfit. That is why all these people who turn up every few years with some patent simplified religion of their own as a substitute for the Christian tradition are really wasting time. Like a man who has no instrument but an old pair of field glasses setting out to put all the real astronomers right. He may be a clever chap—he may be cleverer than some of the real astronomers, but he is not giving himself a chance. And two years later everyone has forgotten all about him, but the real science is still going on.

If Christianity was something we were making up, of course we could make it easier. But it is not. We cannot compete, in simplicity, with people who are inventing religions. How could we? We are dealing with Fact. Of course anyone can be simple if he has no facts to bother about.

CHAPTER 3

Time and Beyond Time

❖

Iᴛ ɪs ᴀ ᴠᴇʀʏ sɪʟʟʏ idea that in reading a book you must never "skip." All sensible people skip freely when they come to a chapter which they find is going to be no use to them. In this chapter I am going to talk about something which may be helpful to some readers, but which may seem to others merely an unnecessary complication. If you are one of the second sort of readers, then I advise you not to bother about this chapter at all but to turn on to the next.

In the last chapter I had to touch on the subject of prayer, and while that is still fresh in your mind and my own, I should like to deal with a difficulty that some people find about the whole idea of prayer. A man put it to me by saying "I can believe in God all right, but what I cannot swallow is the idea of Him attending to several hundred million human beings who are all addressing Him at the same moment." And I have found that quite a lot of people feel this.

Now, the first thing to notice is that the whole sting of it comes in the words *at the same moment*. Most of us can imagine God attending to any number of applicants if only they came one by one and He had an endless time to do it in. So what is really at the back of this difficulty is the idea of God having to fit too many things into one moment of time.

Well that is of course what happens to us. Our life comes to us moment by moment. One moment disappears before the next comes along: and there is room for very little in each. That is what Time is like. And of course you and I tend to take it for granted that this Time series—this arrangement of past, present and future—is not simply the way life comes to us but the way all things really exist. We tend to assume that the whole universe and God Himself are always moving on from past to future just as we do. But many learned men do not agree with that. It was the Theologians who first started the idea that some things are not in Time at all: later the Philosophers took it over: and now some of the scientists are doing the same.

Almost certainly God is not in Time. His life does not consist of moments following one another. If a million people are praying to Him at ten-thirty tonight, He need not listen to them all in that one little snippet which we call ten-thirty. Ten-thirty—and every other moment from the beginning of the world—is always the Present for Him. If you like to put it that way, He has all eternity in which to listen to the split second of prayer put up by a pilot as his plane crashes in flames.

That is difficult, I know. Let me try to give something, not the same, but a bit like it. Suppose I am writing a novel. I write "Mary laid down her work; next moment came a knock at the door!" For Mary who has to live in the imaginary time of my story there is no interval between putting down the work and hearing the knock. But I, who am Mary's maker, do not live in that imaginary time at all. Between writing the first half of that sentence and the second, I might sit down for three hours and think steadily about Mary. I could think about Mary as if she were the only character in the book and for as long as I pleased, and the hours I spent in doing so would not appear in Mary's time (the time inside the story) at all.

This is not a perfect illustration, of course. But it may give just a glimpse of what I believe to be the truth. God is not

hurried along in the Time-stream of this universe any more
than an author is hurried along in the imaginary time of his
own novel. He has infinite attention to spare for each one of
us. He does not have to deal with us in the mass. You are as
much alone with Him as if you were the only being He had
ever created. When Christ died, He died for you individually
just as much as if you had been the only man in the world.

The way in which my illustration breaks down is this. In it
the author gets out of one Time-series (that of the novel) only
by going into another Time-series (the real one). But God, I
believe, does not live in a Time-series at all. His life is not
dribbled out moment by moment like ours: with Him it is, so
to speak, still 1920 and already 1960. For His life is Himself.

If you picture Time as a straight line along which we have
to travel, then you must picture God as the whole page on
which the line is drawn. We come to the parts of the line one
by one: we have to leave A behind before we get to B, and
cannot reach C until we leave B behind. God, from above or
outside or all round, contains the whole line, and sees it all.

The idea is worth trying to grasp because it removes some
apparent difficulties in Christianity. Before I became a Christian one of my objections was as follows. The Christians said
that the eternal God who is everywhere and keeps the whole
universe going, once became a human being. Well then, said
I, how did the whole universe keep going while He was a
baby, or while He was asleep? How could He at the same time
be God who knows everything and also a man asking his disciples "Who touched me?" You will notice that the sting lay in
the *time* words: *"While* He was a baby"—"How could He *at
the same time?"* In other words I was assuming that Christ's
life as God was in time, and that His life as the man Jesus in
Palestine was a shorter period taken out of that time—just as
my service in the army was a shorter period taken out of my
total life. And that is how most of us perhaps tend to think
about it. We picture God living through a period when His
human life was still in the future: then coming to a period

when it was present: then going on to a period when He could look back on it as something in the past. But probably these ideas correspond to nothing in the actual facts. You cannot fit Christ's earthly life in Palestine into any time-relations with His life as God beyond all space and time. It is really, I suggest, a timeless truth about God that human nature, and the human experience of weakness and sleep and ignorance, are somehow included in His whole divine life. This human life in God is from our point of view a particular period in the history of our world (from the year A.D. one till the Crucifixion). We therefore imagine it is also a period in the history of God's own existence. But God has no history. He is too completely and utterly real to have one. For, of course, to have a history means losing part of your reality (because it had already slipped away into the past) and not yet having another part (because it is still in the future): in fact having nothing but the tiny little present, which has gone before you can speak about it. God forbid we should think God was like that. Even we may hope not to be always rationed in that way.

Another difficulty we get if we believe God to be in time is this. Everyone who believes in God at all believes that He knows what you and I are going to do tomorrow. But if He knows I am going to do so-and-so, how can I be free to do otherwise? Well, here once again, the difficulty comes from thinking that God is progressing along the Time-line like us: the only difference being that He can see ahead and we cannot. Well, if that were true, if God *foresaw* our acts, it would be very hard to understand how we could be free not to do them. But suppose God is outside and above the Time-line. In that case, what we call "tomorrow" is visible to Him in just the same way as what we call "today." All the days are "Now" for Him. He does not remember you doing things yesterday; He simply sees you doing them, because, though you have lost yesterday, He has not. He does not "foresee" you doing things tomorrow; He simply sees you doing them: because, though tomorrow is not yet there for you, it is for Him. You never supposed that your actions at this moment were any less free because God knows what you are doing. Well, He knows your tomorrow's actions in just the same way—because He is already in tomorrow and can simply watch you. In a sense, He does not know your action till you have done it: but then the moment at which you have done it is already "Now" for Him.

This idea has helped me a good deal. If it does not help you, leave it alone. It is a "Christian idea" in the sense that great and wise Christians have held it and there is nothing in it contrary to Christianity. But it is not in the Bible or any of the creeds. You can be a perfectly good Christian without accepting it, or indeed without thinking of the matter at all.

CHAPTER 4
Good Infection

❖

I BEGIN THIS CHAPTER by asking you to get a certain picture clear in your minds. Imagine two books lying on a table one on top of the other. Obviously the bottom book is keeping the other one up—supporting it. It is because of the underneath book that the top one is resting, say, two inches from the surface of the table instead of touching the table. Let us call the underneath book A and the top one B. The position of A is causing the position of B. That is clear? Now let us imagine—it could not really happen, of course, but it will do for an illustration—let us imagine that both books have been in that position for ever and ever. In that case B's position would always have been resulting from A's position. But all the same, A's position would not have existed before B's position. In other words the result does not come *after* the cause. Of course, results usually do: you eat the cucumber first and have the indigestion afterwards. But it is not so with all causes and results. You will see in a moment why I think this important.

I said a few pages back that God is a Being which contains three Persons while remaining one Being, just as a cube contains six squares while remaining one body. But as soon as I begin trying to explain how these Persons are connected I have to use words which make it sound as if one of them was there before the others. The First Person is called the Father and the Second the Son. We say that the First begets or produces the second; we call it *begetting*, not *making*, because what He produces is of the same kind as Himself. In that way the word Father is the only word to use. But unfortunately it suggests that He is there first—just as a human father exists before his son. But that is not so. There is no before and after about it. And that is why I have spent some time trying to make clear how one thing can be the source, or cause, or origin, of another without being there before it. The Son exists because the Father exists: but there never was a time before the Father produced the Son.

Perhaps the best way to think of it is this. I asked you just now to imagine those two books, and probably most of you did. That is, you made an act of imagination and as a result you had a mental picture. Quite obviously your act of imagining was the cause and the mental picture the result. But that does not mean that you first did the imagining and then got the picture. The moment you did it, the picture was there. Your will was keeping the picture before you all the time. Yet that act of will and the picture began at exactly the same moment and ended at the same moment. If there were a Being who had always existed and had always been imagining one thing, his act would always have been producing a mental picture; but the picture would be just as eternal as the act.

In the same way we must think of the Son always, so to speak, streaming forth from the Father, like light from a lamp, or heat from a fire, or thoughts from a mind. He is the self-expression of the Father—what the Father has to say. And there never was a time when He was not saying it. But have you noticed what is happening? All these pictures of light or heat are making it sound as if the Father and Son were two things instead of two Persons. So that after all, the New Testament picture of a Father and a Son turns out to be much more accurate than anything we try to substitute for it. That is what always happens when you go away from the words of the Bible. It is quite right to go away from them for a moment in order to make some special point clear. But you must always go back. Naturally God knows how to describe Himself much better than we know how to describe Him. He knows that Father and Son is more like the relation between the First and Second Persons than anything else we can think of. Much the most important thing to know is that it is a relation of love. The Father delights in His Son; the Son looks up to His Father.

Before going on, notice the practical importance of this. All sorts of people are fond of repeating the Christian statement that "God is love." But they seem not to notice that the words "God is love" have no real meaning unless God contains at least two Persons. Love is something that one person has for another person. If God was a single person, then before the world was made, He was not love. Of course, what these people mean when they say that God is love is often something quite different: they really mean "Love is God." They really mean that our feelings of love, however and wherever they arise, and whatever results they produce, are to be treated with great respect. Perhaps they are: but that is something quite different from what Christians mean by the statement "God is love." They believe that the living, dynamic activity of love has been going on in God for ever and has created everything else.

And that, by the way, is perhaps the most important difference between Christianity and all other religions: that in Christianity God is not a static thing—not even a person—but a dynamic, pulsating activity, a life, almost a kind of drama. Almost, if you will not think me irreverent, a kind of dance. The union between the Father and Son is such a live concrete thing that this union itself is also a Person. I know this is almost inconceivable, but look at it thus. You know that among human beings, when they get together in a family, or a club, or a trade union, people talk about the "spirit" of the family, or club, or trade union. They talk about its "spirit" because the individual members, when they are together, do really develop particular ways of talking and behaving which they would not have if they were apart.* It is as if a sort of communal personality came into existence. Of course, it is not a real person: it is only rather like a person. But that is just one of the differences between God and us. What grows out of the joint life of the Father and Son is a real Person, is in fact the Third of the three Persons who are God.

This third Person is called, in technical language, the Holy Ghost or the "spirit" of God. Do not be worried or surprised if you find it (or Him) rather vaguer or more shadowy in your mind than the other two. I think there is a reason why that must be so. In the Christian life you are not usually looking *at* Him: He is always acting through you. If you think of the Father as something "out there," in front of you, and of the Son as someone standing at your side, helping you to pray, trying to turn you into another son, then you have to think of the third Person as something inside you, or behind you. Perhaps some people might find it easier to begin with the third Person and work backwards. God is love, and that love works through men—especially through the whole community of Christians. But this spirit of love is, from all eternity, a love going on between the Father and Son.

And now, what does it all matter? It matters more than anything in the world. The whole dance, or drama, or pattern of this three-Personal life is to be played out in each one of us: or (putting it the other way round) each one of us has got to enter that pattern, take his place in that dance. There is no other way to the happiness for which we were made. Good things as well as bad, you know, are caught by a kind of infection. If you want to get warm you must stand near the fire: if you want to be wet you must get into the water. If you want joy, power, peace, eternal life, you must get close to, or even into, the thing that has them. They are not a sort of prizes

---

*This corporate behaviour may, of course, be either better or worse than their individual behaviour.

which God could if He chose, just hand out to anyone. They are a great fountain of energy and beauty spurting up at the very centre of reality. If you are close to it, the spray will wet you: if you are not, you will remain dry. Once a man is united to God, how could he not live forever? Once a man is separated from God, what can he do but wither and die?

But how is he to be united to God? How is it possible for us to be taken into the three-Personal life?

You remember what I said in Chapter 1 about *begetting* and *making*. We are not begotten by God, we are only made by Him: in our natural state we are not sons of God, only (so to speak) statues. We have not got *Zoe* or spiritual life: only *Bios* or biological life which is presently going to run down and die. Now the whole offer which Christianity makes is this: that we can, if we let God have His way, come to share in the life of Christ. If we do, we shall then be sharing a life which was begotten, not made, which always has existed and always will exist. Christ is the Son of God. If we share in this kind of life we also shall be sons of God. We shall love the Father as He does and the Holy Ghost will arise in us. He came to this world and became a man in order to spread to other men the kind of life He has—by what I call "good infection." Every Christian is to become a little Christ. The whole purpose of becoming a Christian is simply nothing else.

CHAPTER 5

The Obstinate Toy Soldiers

THE SON OF GOD became a man to enable men to become sons of God. We do not know—anyway, *I* do not know—how things would have worked if the human race had never rebelled against God and joined the enemy. Perhaps every man would have been "in Christ," would have shared the life of the Son of God, from the moment he was born. Perhaps the *Bios* or natural life would have been drawn up into the *Zoe*, the uncreated life, at once and as a matter of course. But that is guesswork. You and I are concerned with the way things work now.

And the present state of things is this. The two kinds of life are now not only different (they would always have been that) but actually opposed. The natural life in each of us is something self-centred, something that wants to be petted and admired, to take advantage of other lives, to exploit the whole universe. And especially it wants to be left to itself: to keep well away from anything better or stronger or higher than it, anything that might make it feel small. It is afraid of the light and air of the spiritual world, just as people who have been brought up to be dirty are afraid of a bath. And in a sense it is quite right. It knows that if the spiritual life gets hold of it, all its self-centredness and self-will are going to be killed and it is ready to fight tooth and nail to avoid that.

Did you ever think, when you were a child, what fun it would be if your toys could come to life? Well suppose you could really have brought them to life. Imagine turning a tin soldier into a real little man. It would involve turning the tin into flesh. And suppose the tin soldier did not like it. He is not interested in flesh; all he sees is that the tin is being spoilt. He thinks you are killing him. He will do everything he can to prevent you. He will not be made into a man if he can help it.

What you would have done about that tin soldier I do not know. But what God did about us was this. The Second Person in God, the Son, became human Himself: was born into the world as an actual man—a real man of a particular height, with hair of a particular colour, speaking a particular language, weighing so many stone. The Eternal Being, who knows everything and who created the whole universe, became not only a man but (before that) a baby, and before that a *fœtus* inside a Woman's body. If you want to get the hang of it, think how you would like to become a slug or a crab.

The result of this was that you now had one man who really was what all men were intended to be: one man in whom the created life, derived from his Mother, allowed itself to be completely and perfectly turned into the begotten life. The natural human creature in Him was taken up fully into the divine Son. Thus in one instance humanity had, so to speak, arrived: had passed into the life of Christ. And because the whole difficulty for us is that the natural life has to be, in a sense, "killed," He chose an earthly career which involved the killing of His human desires at every turn—poverty, misunderstanding from His own family, betrayal by one of His intimate friends, being jeered at and manhandled by the Police, and execution by torture. And then, after being thus killed—killed every day in a sense—the human creature in Him, because it was united to the divine Son, came to life again. The Man in Christ rose again: not only the God. That is the whole point. For the first time we saw a real man. One tin soldier—real tin, just like the rest—had come fully and splendidly alive.

And here, of course, we come to the point where my illustration about the tin soldier breaks down. In the case of real toy soldiers or statues, if one came to life, it would obviously make no difference to the rest. They are all separate. But human beings are not. They look separate because you see them walking about separately. But then, we are so made that we can see only the present moment. If we could see the past, then of course it would look different. For there was a time when every man was part of his mother, and (earlier still) part of his father as well: and when they were part of his grandparents. If you could see humanity spread out in time, as God sees it, it would not look like a lot of separate things dotted about. It would look like one single growing thing—rather like a very complicated tree. Every individual would appear connected with every other. And not only that. Individuals are not really separate from God any more than from one another. Every man, woman, and child all over the world is feeling and breathing at this moment only because God, so to speak, is "keeping him going."

Consequently, when Christ becomes man it is not really as if you could become one particular tin soldier. It is as if something which is always affecting the whole human mass begins, at one point, to affect that whole human mass in a new way. From that point the effect spreads through all mankind. It makes a difference to people who lived before Christ as well as to people who lived after Him. It makes a difference to people who have never heard of Him. It is like dropping into a glass of water one drop of something which gives a new taste or a new colour to the whole lot. But, of course, none of these illustrations really works perfectly. In the long run God is no one but Himself and what He does is like nothing else. You could hardly expect it to be.

What, then, is the difference which He has made to the whole human mass? It is just this; that the business of becoming a son of God, of being turned from a created thing into a begotten thing, of passing over from the temporary biological life into timeless "spiritual" life, has been done for us. Humanity is already "saved" in principle. We individuals have to appropriate that salvation. But the really tough work—the bit we could not have done for ourselves—has been done for us. We have not got to try to climb up into spiritual life by our own efforts; it has already come down into the human race. If we will only lay ourselves open to the one Man in whom it was fully present, and who, in spite of being God, is also a real man, He will do it in us and for us. Remember what I said about "good infection." One of our own race has this new life: if we get close to Him we shall catch it from Him.

Of course, you can express this in all sorts of different ways. You can say that Christ died for our sins. You may say that the Father has forgiven us because Christ has done for us what we ought to have done. You may say that we are washed in the blood of the Lamb. You may say that Christ has defeated death. They are all true. If any of them do not appeal to you, leave it alone and get on with the formula that does. And, whatever you do, do not start quarrelling with other people because they use a different formula from yours.

CHAPTER 6
Two Notes

❇

I<small>N ORDER TO AVOID MISUNDERSTANDING</small> I here add notes on
two points arising out of the last chapter.

(1) One sensible critic wrote asking me why, if God wanted
sons instead of "toy soldiers," He did not *beget* many sons at
the outset instead of first *making* toy soldiers and then bringing them to life by such a difficult and painful process. One
part of the answer to this question is fairly easy: the other part
is probably beyond all human knowledge. The easy part is
this. The process of being turned from a creature into a son
would not have been difficult or painful if the human race had
not turned away from God centuries ago. They were able to
do this because He gave them free will: He gave them free will
because a world of mere automata could never love and therefore never know infinite happiness. The difficult part is this.
All Christians are agreed that there is, in the full and original
sense, only one "Son of God." If we insist on asking "But
could there have been many?" we find ourselves in very deep
water. Have the words "Could have been" any sense at all
when applied to God? You can say that one particular finite
thing "could have been" different from what it is, because it
would have been different if something else had been different, and the something else would have been different if some

third thing had been different, and so on. (The letters on this page would have been red if the printer had used red ink, and he would have used red ink if he had been instructed to, and so on.) But when you are talking about God—i.e. about the rock bottom, irreducible Fact on which all other facts depend—it is nonsensical to ask if It could have been otherwise. It is what It is, and there is an end of the matter. But quite apart from this, I find a difficulty about the very idea of the Father begetting many sons from all eternity. In order to be many they would have to be somehow different from one another. Two pennies have the same shape. How are they two? By occupying different places and containing different atoms. In other words, to think of them as different, we have had to bring in space and matter; in fact we have had to bring in "Nature" or the created universe. I can understand the distinction between the Father and the Son without bringing in space or matter, because the one begets and the other is begotten. The Father's relation to the Son is not the same as the Son's relation to the Father. But if there were several sons they would all be related to one another and to the Father in the same way. How would they differ from one another? One does not notice the difficulty at first, of course. One thinks one can form the idea of several "sons." But when I think closely, I find that the idea seemed possible only because I was vaguely imagining them as human forms standing about together in some kind of space. In other words, though I pretended to be thinking about something that exists before any universe was made, I was really smuggling in the picture of a universe and putting that something *inside* it. When I stop doing that and still try to think of the Father begetting many sons "before all worlds" I find I am not really thinking of anything. The idea fades away into mere words. (Was Nature—space and time and matter—created precisely in order to make many-ness possible? Is there perhaps no other way of getting many eternal spirits except by first making many natural creatures, in a universe, and then spiritualising them? But of course all this is guesswork.)

(2) The idea that the whole human race is, in a sense, one thing—one huge organism, like a tree—must not be confused with the idea that individual differences do not matter or that real people, Tom and Nobby and Kate, are somehow less important than collective things like classes, races, and so forth. Indeed the two ideas are opposites. Things which are parts of a single organism may be very different from one another: things which are not, may be very alike. Six pennies are quite separate and very alike: my nose and my lungs are very different but they are only alive at all because they are parts of my body and share its common life. Christianity thinks of human individuals not as mere members of a group or items in a list, but as organs in a body—different from one another and each contributing what no other could. When you find yourself wanting to turn your children, or pupils, or even your neighbours, into people exactly like yourself, remember that God probably never meant them to be that. You and they are different organs, intended to do different things. On the other hand, when you are tempted not to bother about someone else's troubles because they are "no business of yours," remember that though he is different from you he is part of the same organism as you. If you forget that he belongs to the same organism as yourself you will become an Individualist. If you forget that he is a different organ from you, if you want to suppress differences and make people all alike, you will become a Totalitarian. But a Christian must not be either a Totalitarian or an Individualist.

I feel a strong desire to tell you—and I expect you feel a strong desire to tell me—which of these two errors is the worse. That is the devil getting at us. He always sends errors into the world in pairs—pairs of opposites. And he always encourages us to spend a lot of time thinking which is the worse. You see why, of course? He relies on your extra dislike of the one error to draw you gradually into the opposite one. But do not let us be fooled. We have to keep our eyes on the goal and go straight through between both errors. We have no other concern than that with either of them.

CHAPTER 7
Let's Pretend

❋

Mᴀʏ I ᴏɴᴄᴇ ᴀɢᴀɪɴ sᴛᴀʀᴛ by putting two pictures, or two stories rather, into your minds? One is the story you have all read called *Beauty and the Beast*. The girl, you remember, had to marry a monster for some reason. And she did. She kissed it as if it were a man. And then, much to her relief, it really turned into a man and all went well. The other story is about someone who had to wear a mask; a mask which made him look much nicer than he really was. He had to wear it for years. And when he took it off he found his own face had grown to fit it. He was now really beautiful. What had begun as disguise had become a reality. I think both these stories may (in a fanciful way, of course) help to illustrate what I have to say in this chapter. Up till now, I have been trying to describe facts—what God is and what He has done. Now I want to talk about practice—what do we do next? What difference does all this theology make? It can start making a difference tonight. If you are interested enough to have read thus far you are probably interested enough to make a shot at saying your prayers: and, whatever else you say, you will probably say the Lord's Prayer.

Its very first words are *Our Father*. Do you now see what those words mean? They mean quite frankly, that you are putting yourself in the place of a son of God. To put it bluntly, you are *dressing up as Christ*. If you like, you are pretending. Because, of course, the moment you realise what the words mean, you realise that you are not a son of God. You are not being like The Son of God, whose will and interests are at one with those of the Father: you are a bundle of self-centred fears, hopes, greeds, jealousies, and self-conceit, all doomed to death. So that, in a way, this dressing up as Christ is a piece of outrageous cheek. But the odd thing is that He has ordered us to do it.

Why? What is the good of pretending to be what you are not? Well, even on the human level, you know, there are two kinds of pretending. There is a bad kind, where the pretence is there instead of the real thing; as when a man pretends he is going to help you instead of really helping you. But there is also a good kind, where the pretence leads up to the real thing. When you are not feeling particularly friendly but know you ought to be, the best thing you can do, very often, is to put on a friendly manner and behave as if you were a nicer person than you actually are. And in a few minutes, as we have all noticed, you will be really feeling friendlier than you were. Very often the only way to get a quality in reality is to start behaving as if you had it already. That is why children's games are so important. They are always pretending to be grown-ups—playing soldiers, playing shop. But all the time, they are hardening their muscles and sharpening their wits, so that the pretence of being grown-up helps them to grow up in earnest.

Now, the moment you realise "Here I am, dressing up as Christ," it is extremely likely that you will see at once some way in which at that very moment the pretence could be made less of a pretence and more of a reality. You will find several things going on in your mind which would not be going on there if you were really a son of God. Well, stop them. Or you may realise that, instead of saying your prayers, you ought to be downstairs writing a letter, or helping your wife to wash-up. Well, go and do it.

You see what is happening. The Christ Himself, the Son of God who is man (just like you) and God (just like His Father) is actually at your side and is already at that moment beginning to turn your pretence into a reality. This is not merely a fancy way of saying that your conscience is telling you what to do. If you simply ask your conscience, you get one result: if you remember that you are dressing up as Christ, you get a different one. There are lots of things which your conscience might not call definitely wrong (specially things in your mind) but which you will see at once you cannot go on doing if you are seriously trying to be like Christ. For you are no longer thinking simply about right and wrong; you are trying to catch the good infection from a Person. It is more like painting a portrait than like obeying a set of rules. And the odd thing is that while in one way it is much harder than keeping rules, in another way it is far easier.

The real Son of God is at your side. He is beginning to turn you into the same kind of thing as Himself. He is beginning, so to speak, to "inject" His kind of life and thought, His *Zoe*, into you; beginning to turn the tin soldier into a live man. The part of you that does not like it is the part that is still tin.

Some of you may feel that this is very unlike your own experience. You may say "I've never had the sense of being helped by an invisible Christ, but I often have been helped by other human beings." That is rather like the woman in the first war who said that if there were a bread shortage it would not bother her house because they always ate toast. If there is no bread there will be no toast. If there were no help from Christ, there would be no help from other human beings. He works on us in all sorts of ways: not only through what we think our "religious life." He works through Nature, through our own bodies, through books, sometimes through experiences which seem (at the time) *anti*-Christian. When a young man who has been going to church in a routine way honestly realises that he does not believe in Christianity and stops going—provided he does it for honesty's sake and not just to annoy his parents—the spirit of Christ is probably nearer to

him then than it ever was before. But above all, He works on
us through each other.

Men are mirrors, or "carriers" of Christ to other men. Sometimes unconscious carriers. This "good infection" can be carried by those who have not got it themselves. People who
were not Christians themselves helped me to Christianity. But
usually it is those who know Him that bring Him to others.
That is why the Church, the whole body of Christians showing Him to one another, is so important. You might say that
when two Christians are following Christ together there is not
twice as much Christianity as when they are apart, but sixteen
times as much.

But do not forget this. At first it is natural for a baby to take
its mother's milk without knowing its mother. It is equally
natural for us to see the man who helps us without seeing
Christ behind him. But we must not remain babies. We must
go on to recognise the real Giver. It is madness not to. Because, if we do not, we shall be relying on human beings. And
that is going to let us down. The best of them will make mistakes; all of them will die. We must be thankful to all the people who have helped us, we must honour them and love them.
But never, never pin your whole faith on any human being:
not if he is the best and wisest in the whole world. There are
lots of nice things you can do with sand; but do not try building a house on it.

And now we begin to see what it is that the New Testament
is always talking about. It talks about Christians "being born
again"; it talks about them "putting on Christ"; about Christ
"being formed in us"; about our coming to "have the mind of
Christ."

Put right out of your head the idea that these are only fancy
ways of saying that Christians are to read what Christ said
and try to carry it out—as a man may read what Plato or Marx
said and try to carry it out. They mean something much more
than that. They mean that a real Person, Christ, here and now,
in that very room where you are saying your prayers, is doing

things to you. It is not a question of a good man who died two thousand years ago. It is a living Man, still as much a man as you, and still as much God as He was when He created the world, really coming and interfering with your very self; killing the old natural self in you and replacing it with the kind of self He has. At first, only for moments. Then for longer periods. Finally, if all goes well, turning you permanently into a different sort of thing; into a new little Christ, a being which, in its own small way, has the same kind of life as God; which shares in His power, joy, knowledge and eternity. And soon we make two other discoveries.

(1) We begin to notice, besides our particular sinful acts, our sinfulness; begin to be alarmed not only about what we do, but about what we are. This may sound rather difficult, so I will try to make it clear from my own case. When I come to my evening prayers and try to reckon up the sins of the day, nine times out of ten the most obvious one is some sin against charity; I have sulked or snapped or sneered or snubbed or stormed. And the excuse that immediately springs to my mind is that the provocation was so sudden and unexpected: I was caught off my guard, I had not time to collect myself. Now that may be an extenuating circumstance as regards those particular acts: they would obviously be worse if they had been deliberate and premeditated. On the other hand, surely what a man does when he is taken off his guard is the best evidence for what sort of a man he is? Surely what pops out before the man has time to put on a disguise is the truth? If there are rats in a cellar you are most likely to see them if you go in very suddenly. But the suddenness does not create the rats: it only prevents them from hiding. In the same way the suddenness of the provocation does not make me an ill-tempered man: it only shows me what an ill-tempered man I am. The rats are always there in the cellar, but if you go in shouting and noisily they will have taken cover before you switch on the light. Apparently the rats of resentment and vindictiveness are always there in the cellar of my soul. Now that cellar is out

of reach of my conscious will. I can to some extent control my acts: I have no direct control over my temperament. And if (as I said before) what we are matters even more than what we do—if, indeed, what we do matters chiefly as evidence of what we are—then it follows that the change which I most need to undergo is a change that my own direct, voluntary efforts cannot bring about. And this applies to my good actions too. How many of them were done for the right motive? How many for fear of public opinion, or a desire to show off? How many from a sort of obstinacy or sense of superiority which, in different circumstances, might equally have led to some very bad act? But I cannot, by direct moral effort, give myself new motives. After the first few steps in the Christian life we realise that everything which really needs to be done in our souls can be done only by God. And that brings us to something which has been very misleading in my language up to now.

(2) I have been talking as if it were we who did everything. In reality, of course, it is God who does everything. We, at most, allow it to be done to us. In a sense you might even say it is God who does the pretending. The Three-Personal God, so to speak, sees before Him in fact a self-centred, greedy, grumbling, rebellious human animal. But He says "Let us pretend that this is not a mere creature, but our Son. It is like Christ in so far as it is a Man, for He became Man. Let us pretend that it is also like Him in Spirit. Let us treat it as if it were what in fact it is not. Let us pretend in order to make the pretence into a reality." God looks at you as if you were a little Christ: Christ stands beside you to turn you into one. I daresay this idea of a divine make-believe sounds rather strange at first. But, is it so strange really? Is not that how the higher thing always raises the lower? A mother teaches her baby to talk by talking to it as if it understood long before it really does. We treat our dogs as if they were "almost human": that is why they really become "almost human" in the end.

CHAPTER 8

Is Christianity Hard or Easy?

I N THE LAST CHAPTER we were considering the Christian idea of "putting on Christ," or first "dressing up" as a son of God in order that you may finally become a real son. What I want to make clear is that this is not one among many jobs a Christian has to do; and it is not a sort of special exercise for the top class. It is the whole of Christianity. Christianity offers nothing else at all. And I should like to point out how it differs from ordinary ideas of "morality" and "being good."

The ordinary idea which we all have before we become Christians is this. We take as starting point our ordinary self with its various desires and interests. We then admit that something else—call it "morality" or "decent behaviour," or "the good of society"—has claims on this self: claims which interfere with its own desires. What we mean by "being good" is giving in to those claims. Some of the things the ordinary self wanted to do turn out to be what we call "wrong": well, we must give them up. Other things, which the self did not want to do, turn out to be what we call "right": well, we shall have to do them. But we are hoping all the time that when all the demands have been met, the poor natural self will still have some chance, and some time, to get on with its own life and do what it likes. In fact, we are very like an honest man paying his taxes. He pays them all right, but he does hope that there will be enough left over for him to live on. Because we are still taking our natural self as the starting point.

As long as we are thinking that way, one or other of two results is likely to follow. Either we give up trying to be good, or else we become very unhappy indeed. For, make no mistake: if you are really going to try to meet all the demands made on the natural self, it will not have enough left over to live on. The more you obey your conscience, the more your conscience will demand of you. And your natural self, which is thus being starved and hampered and worried at every turn, will get angrier and angrier. In the end, you will either give up trying to be good, or else become one of those people who, as they say, "live for others" but always in a discontented, grumbling way—always wondering why the others do not notice it more and always making a martyr of yourself. And once you have become that you will be a far greater pest to anyone who has to live with you than you would have been if you had remained frankly selfish.

The Christian way is different: harder, and easier. Christ says "Give me All. I don't want so much of your time and so much of your money and so much of your work: I want You. I have not come to torment your natural self, but to kill it. No half-measures are any good. I don't want to cut off a branch here and a branch there, I want to have the whole tree down. I don't want to drill the tooth, or crown it, or stop it, but to have it out. Hand over the whole natural self, all the desires which you think innocent as well as the ones you think wicked—the whole outfit. I will give you a new self instead. In fact, I will give you Myself: my own will shall become yours."

Both harder and easier than what we are all trying to do. You have noticed, I expect, that Christ Himself sometimes describes the Christian way as very hard, sometimes as very easy. He says, "Take up your Cross"—in other words, it is like going to be beaten to death in a concentration camp. Next minute He says, "My yoke is easy and my burden light." He means both. And one can just see why both are true.

Teachers will tell you that the laziest boy in the class is the one who works hardest in the end. They mean this. If you give two boys, say, a proposition in geometry to do, the one who is prepared to take trouble will try to understand it. The lazy boy will try to learn it by heart because, for the moment, that needs less effort. But six months later, when they are preparing for an exam., that lazy boy is doing hours and hours of miserable drudgery over things the other boy understands, and positively enjoys, in a few minutes. Laziness means more work in the long run. Or look at it this way. In a battle, or in mountain climbing, there is often one thing which it takes a lot of pluck to do; but it is also, in the long run, the safest thing to do. If you funk it, you will find yourself, hours later, in far worse danger. The cowardly thing is also the most dangerous thing.

It is like that here. The terrible thing, the almost impossible thing, is to hand over your whole self—all your wishes and precautions—to Christ. But it is far easier than what we are all trying to do instead. For what we are trying to do is to remain what we call "ourselves," to keep personal happiness as our great aim in life, and yet at the same time be "good." We are all trying to let our mind and heart go their own way—centred on money or pleasure or ambition—and hoping, in spite of this, to behave honestly and chastely and humbly. And that is exactly what Christ warned us you could not do. As He said, a thistle cannot produce figs. If I am a field that contains nothing but grass-seed, I cannot produce wheat. Cutting the grass may keep it short: but I shall still produce grass and no wheat. If I want to produce wheat, the change must go deeper than the surface. I must be ploughed up and re-sown.

That is why the real problem of the Christian life comes where people do not usually look for it. It comes the very moment you wake up each morning. All your wishes and hopes for the day rush at you like wild animals. And the first job each morning consists simply in shoving them all back; in listening to that other voice, taking that other point of view, letting that other larger, stronger, quieter life come flowing in. And so on, all day. Standing back from all your natural fussings and frettings; coming in out of the wind.

We can only do it for moments at first. But from those moments the new sort of life will be spreading through our system: because now we are letting Him work at the right part of us. It is the difference between paint, which is merely laid on the surface, and a dye or stain which soaks right through. He never talked vague, idealistic gas. When he said, "Be perfect," He meant it. He meant that we must go in for the full treatment. It is hard; but the sort of compromise we are all hankering after is harder—in fact, it is impossible. It may be hard for an egg to turn into a bird: it would be a jolly sight harder for it to learn to fly while remaining an egg. We are like eggs at present. And you cannot go on indefinitely being just an ordinary, decent egg. We must be hatched or go bad.

May I come back to what I said before? This is the whole of Christianity. There is nothing else. It is so easy to get muddled about that. It is easy to think that the Church has a lot of different objects—education, building, missions, holding services. Just as it is easy to think the State has a lot of different objects—military, political, economic, and what not. But in a way things are much simpler than that. The State exists simply to promote and to protect the ordinary happiness of human beings in this life. A husband and wife chatting over a fire, a couple of friends having a game of darts in a pub, a man reading a book in his own room or digging in his own garden—that is what the State is there for. And unless they are helping to increase and prolong and protect such moments, all the laws, parliaments, armies, courts, police, economics, etc., are simply a waste of time. In the same way the Church exists for nothing else but to draw men into Christ, to make them little Christs. If they are not doing that, all the cathedrals, clergy, missions, sermons, even the Bible itself, are simply a waste of time. God became Man for no other purpose. It is even doubtful, you know, whether the whole universe was created for any other purpose. It says in the Bible that the whole universe was made for Christ and that everything is to be gathered together in Him. I do not suppose any of us can understand how this will happen as regards the whole universe. We do not know what (if anything) lives in the parts of it that are millions of miles away from this Earth. Even on this Earth we do not know how it applies to things other than men. After all, that is what you would expect. We have been shown the plan only in so far as it concerns ourselves.

I sometimes like to imagine that I can just see how it might apply to other things. I think I can see how the higher animals are in a sense drawn into Man when he loves them and makes them (as he does) much more nearly human than they would otherwise be. I can even see a sense in which the dead things and plants are drawn into Man as he studies them and uses and appreciates them. And if there were intelligent creatures in other worlds they might do the same with their worlds. It might be that when intelligent creatures entered into Christ they would, in that way, bring all the other things in along with them. But I do not know: it is only a guess.

What we have been told is how we men can be drawn into Christ—can become part of that wonderful present which the young Prince of the universe wants to offer to His Father—that present which is Himself and therefore us in Him. It is the only thing we were made for. And there are strange, exciting hints in the Bible that when we are drawn in, a great many other things in Nature will begin to come right. The bad dream will be over: it will be morning.

CHAPTER 9

Counting the Cost

I FIND A GOOD MANY PEOPLE have been bothered by what I said in the last chapter about Our Lord's words, "Be ye perfect." Some people seem to think this means "Unless you are perfect, I will not help you"; and as we cannot be perfect, then, if He meant that, our position is hopeless. But I do not think He did mean that. I think He meant "The only help I will give is help to become perfect. You may want something less: but I will give you nothing less."

Let me explain. When I was a child I often had toothache, and I knew that if I went to my mother she would give me something which would deaden the pain for that night and let me get to sleep. But I did not go to my mother—at least, not till the pain became very bad. And the reason I did not go was this. I did not doubt she would give me the aspirin; but I knew she would also do something else. I knew she would take me to the dentist next morning. I could not get what I wanted out of her without getting something more, which I did not want. I wanted immediate relief from pain: but I could not get it without having my teeth set permanently right. And I knew those dentists; I knew they started fiddling about with all sorts of other teeth which had not yet begun to ache. They would not let sleeping dogs lie; if you gave them an inch they took an ell.

Now, if I may put it that way, Our Lord is like the dentists. If you give Him an inch, He will take an ell. Dozens of people go to Him to be cured of some one particular sin which they are ashamed of (like masturbation or physical cowardice) or which is obviously spoiling daily life (like bad temper or drunkenness). Well, He will cure it all right: but He will not stop there. That may be all you asked; but if once you call Him in, He will give you the full treatment.

That is why He warned people to "count the cost" before becoming Christians. "Make no mistake," He says, "if you let me, I will make you perfect. The moment you put yourself in My hands, that is what you are in for. Nothing less, or other, than that. You have free will, and if you choose, you can push Me away. But if you do not push Me away, understand that I am going to see this job through. Whatever suffering it may cost you in your earthly life, whatever inconceivable purification it may cost you after death, whatever it costs Me, I will never rest, nor let you rest, until you are literally perfect—until my Father can say without reservation that He is well pleased with you, as He said He was well pleased with me. This I can do and will do. But I will not do anything less."

And yet—this is the other and equally important side of it— this Helper who will, in the long run, be satisfied with nothing less than absolute perfection, will also be delighted with the first feeble, stumbling effort you make tomorrow to do the simplest duty. As a great Christian writer (George MacDonald) pointed out, every father is pleased at the baby's first attempt to walk: no father would be satisfied with anything less than a firm, free, manly walk in a grown-up son. In the same way, he said, "God is easy to please, but hard to satisfy."

The practical upshot is this. On the one hand, God's demand for perfection need not discourage you in the least in your present attempts to be good, or even in your present failures. Each time you fall He will pick you up again. And He knows perfectly well that your own efforts are never going to bring you anywhere near perfection. On the other hand, you must realise from the outset that the goal towards which He is beginning to guide you is absolute perfection; and no power in the whole universe, except you yourself, can prevent Him from taking you to that goal. That is what you are in for. And it is very important to realise that. If we do not, then we are very likely to start pulling back and resisting Him after a certain point. I think that many of us, when Christ has enabled us to overcome one or two sins that were an obvious nuisance, are inclined to feel (though we do not put it into words) that we are now good enough. He has done all we wanted Him to do, and we should be obliged if He would now leave us alone. As we say "I never expected to be a saint, I only wanted to be a decent ordinary chap." And we imagine when we say this that we are being humble.

But this is the fatal mistake. Of course we never wanted, and never asked, to be made into the sort of creatures He is going to make us into. But the question is not what we intended ourselves to be, but what He intended us to be when He made us. He is the inventor, we are only the machine. He is the painter, we are only the picture. How should we know what He means us to be like? You see, He has already made us something very different from what we were. Long ago, before we were born, when we were inside our mothers' bodies, we passed through various stages. We were once rather like vegetables, and once rather like fish; it was only at a later stage that we became like human babies. And if we had been conscious at those earlier stages, I daresay we should have been quite contented to stay as vegetables or fish—should not have wanted to be made into babies. But all the time He knew His plan for us and was determined to carry it out. Something the same is now happening at a higher level. We may be content to remain what we call "ordinary people": but He is determined to carry out a quite different plan. To shrink back from that plan is not humility; it is laziness and cowardice. To submit to it is not conceit or megalomania; it is obedience.

Here is another way of putting the two sides of the truth. On the one hand we must never imagine that our own unaided efforts can be relied on to carry us even through the next twenty-four hours as "decent" people. If He does not support us, not one of us is safe from some gross sin. On the other hand, no possible degree of holiness or heroism which has ever been recorded of the greatest saints is beyond what He is determined to produce in every one of us in the end. The job will not be completed in this life: but He means to get us as far as possible before death.

That is why we must not be surprised if we are in for a rough time. When a man turns to Christ and seems to be getting on pretty well (in the sense that some of his bad habits are now corrected), he often feels that it would now be natural if things went fairly smoothly. When troubles come along— illnesses, money troubles, new kinds of temptation—he is disappointed. These things, he feels, might have been necessary to rouse him and make him repent in his bad old days; but why now? Because God is forcing him on, or up, to a higher level: putting him into situations where he will have to be very much braver, or more patient, or more loving, than he ever dreamed of being before. It seems to us all unnecessary: but that is because we have not yet had the slightest notion of the tremendous thing He means to make of us.

I find I must borrow yet another parable from George MacDonald. Imagine yourself as a living house. God comes in to rebuild that house. At first, perhaps, you can understand what He is doing. He is getting the drains right and stopping the leaks in the roof and so on: you knew that those jobs needed doing and so you are not surprised. But presently he starts knocking the house about in a way that hurts abominably and does not seem to make sense. What on earth is He up to? The explanation is that He is building quite a different house from the one you thought of—throwing out a new wing here, putting on an extra floor there, running up towers, making courtyards. You thought you were going to be made into a decent little cottage: but He is building a palace. He intends to come and live in it Himself.

The command *Be ye perfect* is not idealistic gas. Nor is it a command to do the impossible. He is going to make us into creatures that can obey that command. He said (in the Bible) that we were "gods" and He is going to make good His words. If we let Him—for we can prevent Him, if we choose—He will make the feeblest and filthiest of us into a god or goddess, a dazzling, radiant, immortal creature, pulsating all through with such energy and joy and wisdom and love as we cannot now imagine, a bright stainless mirror which reflects back to God perfectly (though, of course, on a smaller scale) His own boundless power and delight and goodness. The process will be long and in parts very painful; but that is what we are in for. Nothing less. He meant what He said.

CHAPTER 10

Nice People or New Men

❈

H E MEANT WHAT HE SAID. Those who put themselves in His hands will become perfect, as He is perfect—perfect in love, wisdom, joy, beauty, and immortality. The change will not be completed in this life, for death is an important part of the treatment. How far the change will have gone before death in any particular Christian is uncertain.

I think this is the right moment to consider a question which is often asked: If Christianity is true why are not all Christians obviously nicer than all non-Christians? What lies behind that question is partly something very reasonable and partly something that is not reasonable at all. The reasonable part is this. If conversion to Christianity makes no improvement in a man's outward actions—if he continues to be just as snobbish or spiteful or envious or ambitious as he was before—then I think we must suspect that his "conversion" was largely imaginary; and after one's original conversion, every time one thinks one has made an advance, that is the test to apply. Fine feelings, new insights, greater interest in "religion" mean nothing unless they make our actual behaviour better; just as in an illness "feeling better" is not much good if the thermometer shows that your temperature is still going up. In that sense the outer world is quite right to judge Christianity by its results. Christ told us to judge by results. A tree is known by its fruit; or, as we say, the proof of the pudding is in the eating. When we Christians behave badly, or fail to behave well, we are making Christianity unbelievable to the outside world. The wartime posters told us that Careless Talk costs Lives. It is equally true that Careless Lives cost Talk. Our careless lives set the outer world talking; and we give them grounds for talking in a way that throws doubt on the truth of Christianity itself.

But there is another way of demanding results in which the outer world may be quite illogical. They may demand not merely that each man's life should improve if he becomes a Christian: they may also demand before they believe in Christianity that they should see the whole world neatly divided into two camps—Christian and non-Christian—and that all the people in the first camp at any given moment should be obviously nicer than all the people in the second. This is unreasonable on several grounds.

(1) In the first place the situation in the actual world is much more complicated than that. The world does not consist of 100 per cent. Christians and 100 per cent. non-Christians. There are people (a great many of them) who are slowly ceasing to be Christians but who still call themselves by that name: some of them are clergymen. There are other people who are slowly becoming Christians though they do not yet call themselves so. There are people who do not accept the full Christian doctrine about Christ but who are so strongly attracted by Him that they are His in a much deeper sense than they themselves understand. There are people in other religions who are being led by God's secret influence to concentrate on those parts of their religion which are in agreement with Christianity, and who thus belong to Christ without knowing it. For example, a Buddhist of good will may be led to concentrate more and more on the Buddhist teaching about mercy and to leave in the background (though he might still say he believed) the Buddhist teaching on certain other points. Many of the good

Pagans long before Christ's birth may have been in this position. And always, of course, there are a great many people
who are just confused in mind and have a lot of inconsistent
beliefs all jumbled up together. Consequently, it is not much
use trying to make judgments about Christians and non-
Christians in the mass. It is some use comparing cats and
dogs, or even men and women, in the mass, because there one
knows definitely which is which. Also, an animal does not
turn (either slowly or suddenly) from a dog into a cat. But
when we are comparing Christians in general with non-
Christians in general, we are usually not thinking about real
people whom we know at all, but only about two vague ideas
which we have got from novels and newspapers. If you want
to compare the bad Christian and the good Atheist, you must
think about two real specimens whom you have actually met.
Unless we come down to brass tacks in that way, we shall only
be wasting time.

(2) Suppose we have come down to brass tacks and are now
talking not about an imaginary Christian and an imaginary
non-Christian, but about two real people in our own neigh-
bourhood. Even then we must be careful to ask the right question. If Christianity is true then it ought to follow (*a*) That any
Christian will be nicer than the same person would be if he
were not a Christian. (*b*) That any man who becomes a Christian will be nicer than he was before. Just in the same way, if
the advertisements of Whitesmile's toothpaste are true it ought
to follow (*a*) That anyone who uses it will have better teeth
than the same person would have if he did not use it. (*b*) That
if anyone begins to use it his teeth will improve. But to point
out that I, who use Whitesmile's (and also have inherited bad
teeth from both my parents), have not got as fine a set as
some healthy young Negro who never used toothpaste at all,
does not, by itself, prove that the advertisements are untrue.
Christian Miss Bates may have an unkinder tongue than unbelieving Dick Firkin. That, by itself, does not tell us
whether Christianity works. The question is what Miss Bates's

tongue would be like if she were not a Christian and what Dick's would be like if he became one. Miss Bates and Dick, as a result of natural causes and early upbringing, have certain temperaments: Christianity professes to put both temperaments under new management if they will allow it to do so. What you have a right to ask is whether that management, if allowed to take over, improves the concern. Everyone knows that what is being managed in Dick Firkin's case is much "nicer" than what is being managed in Miss Bates's. That is not the point. To judge the management of a factory, you must consider not only the output but the plant. Considering the plant at Factory A it may be a wonder that it turns out anything at all; considering the first-class outfit at Factory B its output, though high, may be a great deal lower than it ought to be. No doubt the good manager at Factory A is going to put in new machinery as soon as he can, but that takes time. In the meantime low output does not prove that he is a failure.

(3) And now, let us go a little deeper. The manager is going to put in new machinery: before Christ has finished with Miss Bates, she is going to be very "nice" indeed. But if we left it at that, it would sound as though Christ's only aim was to pull Miss Bates up to the same level on which Dick had been all along. We have been talking, in fact, as if Dick were all right; as if Christianity was something nasty people needed and nice ones could afford to do without; and as if niceness was all that God demanded. But this would be a fatal mistake. The truth is that in God's eyes Dick Firkin needs "saving" every bit as much as Miss Bates. In one sense (I will explain what sense in a moment) niceness hardly comes into the question.

You cannot expect God to look at Dick's placid temper and friendly disposition exactly as we do. They result from natural causes which God Himself creates. Being merely temperamental, they will all disappear if Dick's digestion alters. The niceness, in fact, is God's gift to Dick, not Dick's gift to God. In the same way, God has allowed natural causes, working in a world spoiled by centuries of sin, to produce in Miss Bates

the narrow mind and jangled nerves which account for most
of her nastiness. He intends, in His own good time, to set that
part of her right. But that is not, for God, the critical part of
the business. It presents no difficulties. It is not what He is
anxious about. What He is watching and waiting and working
for is something that is not easy even for God, because, from
the nature of the case, even He cannot produce it by a mere
act of power. He is waiting and watching for it both in Miss
Bates and in Dick Firkin. It is something they can freely give
Him or freely refuse to Him. Will they, or will they not, turn
to Him and thus fulfill the only purpose for which they were
created? Their free will is trembling inside them like the
needle of a compass. But this is a needle that can choose. It
can point to its true North; but it need not. Will the needle
swing round, and settle, and point to God?

He can help it to do so. He cannot force it. He cannot, so to
speak, put out His own hand and pull it into the right position, for then it would not be free will any more. Will it point
North? That is the question on which all hangs. Will Miss
Bates and Dick offer their natures to God? The question
whether the natures they offer or withhold are, at that moment, nice or nasty ones, is of secondary importance. God can
see to that part of the problem.

Do not misunderstand me. Of course God regards a nasty
nature as a bad and deplorable thing. And, of course, He regards a nice nature as a good thing—good like bread, or sun-
shine, or water. But these are the good things which He gives
and we receive. He created Dick's sound nerves and good
digestion, and there is plenty more where they came from. It
costs God nothing, so far as we know, to create nice things:
but to convert rebellious wills cost Him crucifixion. And because they are wills they can—in nice people just as much as
in nasty ones—refuse His request. And then, because that
niceness in Dick was merely part of nature, it will all go to
pieces in the end. Nature herself will all pass away. Natural
causes come together in Dick to make a pleasant psychological

pattern, just as they come together in a sunset to make a pleasant pattern of colours. Presently (for that is how nature works) they will fall apart again and the pattern in both cases will disappear. Dick has had the chance to turn (or rather, to allow God to turn) that momentary pattern into the beauty of an eternal spirit: and he has not taken it.

There is a paradox here. As long as Dick does not turn to God, he thinks his niceness is his own, and just as long as he thinks that, it is not his own. It is when Dick realises that his niceness is not his own but a gift from God, and when he offers it back to God—it is just then that it begins to be really his own. For now Dick is beginning to take a share in his own creation. The only things we can keep are the things we freely give to God. What we try to keep for ourselves is just what we are sure to lose.

We must, therefore, not be surprised if we find among the Christians some people who are still nasty. There is even, when you come to think it over, a reason why nasty people might be expected to turn to Christ in greater numbers than nice ones. That was what people objected to about Christ during His life on earth: He seemed to attract "such awful people." That is what people still object to, and always will. Do you not see why? Christ said "Blessed are the poor" and "How hard it is for the rich to enter the Kingdom," and no doubt He primarily meant the economically rich and economically poor. But do not His words also apply to another kind of riches and poverty? One of the dangers of having a lot of money is that you may be quite satisfied with the kinds of happiness money can give and so fail to realise your need for God. If everything seems to come simply by signing checks, you may forget that you are at every moment totally dependent on God. Now quite plainly, natural gifts carry with them a similar danger. If you have sound nerves and intelligence and health and popularity and a good upbringing, you are likely to be quite satisfied with your character as it is. "Why drag God into it?" you may ask. A certain level of good conduct comes fairly easily to you. You are not one of those wretched creatures who are always being tripped up by sex, or dipsomania, or nervousness, or bad temper. Everyone says you are a nice chap and (between ourselves) you agree with them. You are quite likely to believe that all this niceness is your own doing: and you may easily not feel the need for any better kind of goodness. Often people who have all these natural kinds of goodness cannot be brought to recognise their need for Christ at all until, one day, the natural goodness lets them down and their self-satisfaction is shattered. In other words, it is hard for those who are "rich" in this sense to enter the Kingdom.

It is very different for the nasty people—the little, low, timid, warped, thin-blooded, lonely people, or the passionate, sensual, unbalanced people. If they make any attempt at goodness at all, they learn, in double quick time, that they need help. It is Christ or nothing for them. It is taking up the cross and following—or else despair. They are the lost sheep; He came specially to find them. They are (in one very real and terrible sense) the "poor": He blessed them. They are the "awful set" he goes about with—and of course the Pharisees say still, as they said from the first, "If there were anything in Christianity those people would not be Christians."

There is either a warning or an encouragement here for every one of us. If you are a nice person—if virtue comes easily to you—beware! Much is expected from those to whom much is given. If you mistake for your own merits what are really God's gifts to you through nature, and if you are contented with simply being nice, you are still a rebel: and all those gifts will only make your fall more terrible, your corruption more complicated, your bad example more disastrous. The Devil was an archangel once; his natural gifts were as far above yours as yours are above those of a chimpanzee.

But if you are a poor creature—poisoned by a wretched upbringing in some house full of vulgar jealousies and senseless quarrels—saddled, by no choice of your own, with some loathsome sexual perversion—nagged day in and day out by an inferiority complex that makes you snap at your best friends—do not despair. He knows all about it. You are one of the poor whom He blessed. He knows what a wretched machine you are trying to drive. Keep on. Do what you can. One day (perhaps in another world, but perhaps far sooner than that) he will fling it on the scrap-heap and give you a new one. And then you may astonish us all—not least yourself: for you have learned your driving in a hard school. (Some of the last will be first and some of the first will be last.)

"Niceness"—wholesome, integrated personality—is an excellent thing. We must try by every medical, educational, economic, and political means in our power, to produce a world where as many people as possible grow up "nice"; just as we must try to produce a world where all have plenty to eat. But we must not suppose that even if we succeeded in making everyone nice we should have saved their souls. A world of nice people, content in their own niceness, looking no further, turned away from God, would be just as desperately in need of salvation as a miserable world—and might even be more difficult to save.

For mere improvement is not redemption, though redemption always improves people even here and now and will, in the end, improve them to a degree we cannot yet imagine. God became man to turn creatures into sons: not simply to produce better men of the old kind but to produce a new kind of man. It is not like teaching a horse to jump better and better but like turning a horse into a winged creature. Of course, once it has got its wings, it will soar over fences which could never have been jumped and thus beat the natural horse at its own game. But there may be a period, while the wings are just beginning to grow, when it cannot do so: and at that stage the lumps on the shoulders—no one could tell by looking at them that they are going to be wings—may even give it an awkward appearance.

But perhaps we have already spent too long on this question. If what you want is an argument against Christianity (and I well remember how eagerly I looked for such arguments when I began to be afraid it was true) you can easily find some stupid and unsatisfactory Christian and say, "So there's your boasted new man! Give me the old kind." But if once you have begun to see that Christianity is on other grounds probable, you will know in your heart that this is only evading the issue. What can you ever really know of other people's souls—of their temptations, their opportunities, their struggles? One soul in the whole creation you do know: and it is the only one whose fate is placed in your hands. If there is a God, you are, in a sense, alone with Him. You cannot put Him off with speculations about your next door neighbours or memories of what you have read in books. What will all that chatter and hearsay count (will you even be able to remember it?) when the anæsthetic fog which we call "nature" or "the real world" fades away and the Presence in which you have always stood becomes palpable, immediate, and unavoidable?

CHAPTER 11

The New Men

❖

In the last chapter I compared Christ's work of making New Men to the process of turning a horse into a winged creature. I used that extreme example in order to emphasise the point that it is not mere improvement but Transformation. The nearest parallel to it in the world of nature is to be found in the remarkable transformations we can make in insects by applying certain rays to them. Some people think this is how Evolution worked. The alterations in creatures on which it all depends may have been produced by rays coming from outer space. (Of course once the alterations are there, what they call "Natural Selection" gets to work on them: i.e. the useful alterations survive and the other ones get weeded out.)

Perhaps a modern man can understand the Christian idea best if he takes it in connection with Evolution. Everyone now knows about Evolution (though, of course, some educated people disbelieve it): everyone has been told that man has evolved from lower types of life. Consequently, people often wonder "What is the next step? When is the thing beyond man going to appear?" Imaginative writers try sometimes to picture this next step—the "Superman" as they call him; but they usually only succeed in picturing someone a good deal nastier than man as we know him and then try to make up for that by sticking on extra legs or arms. But supposing the next step was to be something even more different from the earlier steps than they ever dreamed of? And is it not very likely it would be? Thousands of centuries ago huge, very heavily armoured creatures were evolved. If anyone had at that time been watching the course of Evolution he would probably have expected that it was going to go on to heavier and heavier armour. But he would have been wrong. The future had a card up its sleeve which nothing at that time would have led him to expect. It was going to spring on him little, naked, unarmoured animals which had better brains: and with those brains they were going to master the whole planet. They were not merely going to have more power than the prehistoric monsters, they were going to have a new kind of power. The next step was not only going to be different, but different with a new kind of difference. The stream of Evolution was not going to flow on in the direction in which he saw it flowing: it was in fact going to take a sharp bend.

Now it seems to me that most of the popular guesses at the Next Step are making just the same sort of mistake. People see (or at any rate they think they see) men developing greater brains and getting greater mastery over nature. And because they think the stream is flowing in that direction, they imagine it will go on flowing in that direction. But I cannot help thinking that the Next Step will be really new; it will go off in a direction you could never have dreamed of. It would hardly be worth calling a New Step unless it did. I should expect not merely difference but a new kind of difference. I should expect not merely change but a new method of producing the change. Or, to make an Irish bull, I should expect the next stage in Evolution not to be a stage in Evolution at all: should expect the Evolution itself as a method of producing change, will be superseded. And finally, I should not be surprised if, when the thing happened, very few people noticed that it was happening.

Now, if you care to talk in these terms, the Christian view

is precisely that the Next Step has already appeared. And it is really new. It is not a change from brainy men to brainier men: it is a change that goes off in a totally different direction—a change from being creatures of God to being sons of God. The first instance appeared in Palestine two thousand years ago. In a sense, the change is not "Evolution" at all, because it is not something arising out of the natural process of events but something coming into nature from outside. But that is what I should expect. We arrived at our idea of "Evolution" from studying the past. If there are real novelties in store then of course our idea, based on the past, will not really cover them. And in fact this New Step differs from all previous ones not only in coming from outside nature but in several other ways as well.

(1) It is not carried on by sexual reproduction. Need we be surprised at that? There was a time before sex had appeared; development used to go on by different methods. Consequently, we might have expected that there would come a time when sex disappeared, or else (which is what is actually happening) a time when sex, though it continued to exist, ceased to be the main channel of development.

(2) At the earlier stages living organisms have had either no choice or very little choice about taking the new step. Progress was, in the main, something that happened to them, not something that they did. But the new step, the step from being creatures to being sons, is voluntary. At least, voluntary in one sense. It is not voluntary in the sense that we, of ourselves, could have chosen to take it or could even have imagined it; but it is voluntary in the sense that when it is offered to us we can refuse it. We can, if we please, shrink back: we can dig in our heels and let the new Humanity go on without us.

(3) I have called Christ the "first instance" of the new man. But of course He is something much more than that. He is not merely a new man, one specimen of the species, but *the* new man. He is the origin and centre and life of all the new men.

He came into the created universe, of His own will, bringing with Him the *Zoe*, the new life. (I mean new to us, of course: in its own place *Zoe* has existed for ever and ever.) And He transmits it not by heredity but by what I have called "good infection." Everyone who gets it gets it by personal contact with Him. Other men become "new" by being "in Him."

(4) This step is taken at a different speed from the previous ones. Compared with the development of man on this planet, the diffusion of Christianity over the human race seems to go like a flash of lightning—for two thousand years is almost nothing in the history of the universe. (Never forget that we are all still "the early Christians." The present wicked and wasteful divisions between us are, let us hope, a disease of infancy: we are still teething. The outer world, no doubt, thinks just the opposite. It thinks we are dying of old age. But it has thought that so often before! Again and again it has thought Christianity was dying, dying by persecutions from without or corruptions from within, by the rise of Mohammedanism, the rise of the physical sciences, the rise of great anti-Christian revolutionary movements. But every time the world has been disappointed. Its first disappointment was over the crucifixion. The Man came to life again. In a sense— and I quite realise how frightfully unfair it must seem to them—that has been happening ever since. They keep on killing the thing that He started: and each time, just as they are patting down the earth on its grave, they suddenly hear that it is still alive and has even broken out in some new place. No wonder they hate us.)

(5) The stakes are higher. By falling back at the earlier steps a creature lost, at the worst, its few years of life on this earth: very often it did not lose even that. By falling back at this step we lose a prize which is (in the strictest sense of the word) infinite. For now the critical moment has arrived. Century by century God has guided nature up to the point of producing creatures which can (if they will) be taken right out of nature, turned into "gods." Will they allow themselves to be taken? In

a way, it is like the crisis of birth. Until we rise and follow Christ we are still parts of Nature, still in the womb of our great mother. Her pregnancy has been long and painful and anxious, but it has reached its climax. The great moment has come. Everything is ready. The Doctor has arrived. Will the birth "go off all right"? But of course it differs from an ordinary birth in one important respect. In an ordinary birth the baby has not much choice: here it has. I wonder what an ordinary baby would do if it had the choice. It might prefer to stay in the dark and warmth and safety of the womb. For of course it would think the womb meant safety. That would be just where it was wrong; for if it stays there it will die.

On this view the thing has happened: the new step has been taken and is being taken. Already the new men are dotted here and there all over the earth. Some, as I have admitted, are still hardly recognisable: but others can be recognised. Every now and then one meets them. Their very voices and faces are different from ours; stronger, quieter, happier, more radiant. They begin where most of us leave off. They are, I say, recognisable; but you must know what to look for. They will not be very like the idea of "religious people" which you have formed from your general reading. They do not draw attention to themselves. You tend to think that you are being kind to them when they are really being kind to you. They love you more than other men do, but they need you less. (We must get over wanting to be needed: in some goodish people, specially women, that is the hardest of all temptations to resist.) They will usually seem to have a lot of time: you will wonder where it comes from. When you have recognised one of them, you will recognise the next one much more easily. And I strongly suspect (but how should I know?) that they recognise one another immediately and infallibly, across every barrier of colour, sex, class, age, and even of creeds. In that way, to become holy is rather like joining a secret society. To put it at the very lowest, it must be great *fun*.

But you must not imagine that the new men are, in the ordinary sense, all alike. A good deal of what I have been saying in this last book might make you suppose that that was bound to be so. To become new men means losing what we now call "ourselves." Out of ourselves, into Christ, we must go. His will is to become ours and we are to think His thoughts, to "have the mind of Christ" as the Bible says. And if Christ is one, and if He is thus to be "in" us all, shall we not be exactly the same? It certainly sounds like it; but in fact it is not so.

It is difficult here to get a good illustration; because, of course, no other two things are related to each other just as the Creator is related to one of His creatures. But I will try two very imperfect illustrations which may give a hint of the truth. Imagine a lot of people who have always lived in the dark. You come and try to describe to them what light is like. You might tell them that if they come into the light that same light would fall on them all and they would all reflect it and thus become what we call visible. Is it not quite possible that they would imagine that, since they were all receiving the same light, and all reacting to it in the same way (i.e. all reflecting it), they would all look alike? Whereas you and I know that the light will in fact bring out, or show up, how different they are. Or again, suppose a person who knew nothing about salt. You give him a pinch to taste and he experiences a particular strong, sharp taste. You then tell him that in your country people use salt in all their cookery. Might he not reply "In that case I suppose all your dishes taste exactly the same: because the taste of that stuff you have just given me is so strong that it will kill the taste of everything else." But you and I know that the real effect of salt is exactly the opposite. So far from killing the taste of the egg and the tripe and the cabbage, it actually brings it out. They do not show their real taste till you have added the salt. (Of course, as I warned you, this is not really a very good illustration, because you can, after all, kill the other tastes by putting in too much salt, whereas you cannot kill the taste of a human personality by putting in too much Christ. I am doing the best I can.)

It is something like that with Christ and us. The more we get what we now call "ourselves" out of the way and let Him take us over, the more truly ourselves we become. There is so much of Him that millions and millions of "little Christs," all different, will still be too few to express Him fully. He made them all. He invented—as an author invents characters in a novel—all the different men that you and I were intended to be. In that sense our real selves are all waiting for us in Him. It is no good trying to "be myself" without Him. The more I resist Him and try to live on my own, the more I become dominated by my own heredity and upbringing and surroundings and natural desires. In fact what I so proudly call "Myself" becomes merely the meeting place for trains of events which I never started and which I cannot stop. What I call "My wishes" become merely the desires thrown up by my physical organism or pumped into me by other men's thoughts or even suggested to me by devils. Eggs and alcohol and a good night's sleep will be the real origins of what I flatter myself by regarding as my own highly personal and discriminating decision to make love to the girl opposite to me in the railway carriage. Propaganda will be the real origin of what I regard as my own personal political ideals. I am not, in my natural state, nearly so much of a person as I like to believe: most of what I call "me" can be very easily explained. It is when I turn to Christ, when I give myself up to His Personality, that I first begin to have a real personality of my own.

At the beginning I said there were Personalities in God. I will go further now. There are no real personalities anywhere else. Until you have given up your self to Him you will not have a real self. Sámeness is to be found most among the most "natural" men, not among those who surrender to Christ. How monotonously alike all the great tyrants and conquerors have been: how gloriously different are the saints.

But there must be a real giving up of the self. You must throw it away "blindly" so to speak. Christ will indeed give you a real personality: but you must not go to Him for the sake of that. As long as your own personality is what you are bothering about you are not going to Him at all. The very first step is to try to forget about the self altogether. Your real, new self (which is Christ's and also yours, and yours just because it is His) will not come as long as you are looking for it. It will come when you are looking for Him. Does that sound strange? The same principle holds, you know, for more everyday matters. Even in social life, you will never make a good impression on other people until you stop thinking about what sort of impression you are making. Even in literature and art, no man who bothers about originality will ever be original: whereas if you simply try to tell the truth (without caring twopence how often it has been told before) you will, nine times out of ten, become original without ever having noticed it. The principle runs through all life from top to bottom. Give up your self, and you will find your real self. Lose your life and you will save it. Submit to death, death of your ambitions and favourite wishes every day and death of your whole body in the end: submit with every fibre of your being, and you will find eternal life. Keep back nothing. Nothing that you have not given away will ever be really yours. Nothing in you that has not died will ever be raised from the dead. Look for yourself, and you will find in the long run only hatred, loneliness, despair, rage, ruin, and decay. But look for Christ and you will find Him, and with Him everything else thrown in.

Classics of the Christian Faith

$\mathfrak{N}$ow available for your church or personal library — classic Christian titles in special, deluxe gift bindings, at a economical price.

The Christian Library has been designed and produced for th discerning book lover. All are outstanding titles, in durable, matchin bindings that will stand up to years of active use.

You would ordinarily expect to pay twice the $5.99 price for books o this quality. Stop at your local bookstore and see the quality of Th Christian Library for yourself.

Begin building your library today, with books from The Christia Library.

Titles Available $5.99 each*

Abide in Christ   Andrew Murray
Absolute Surrender   Andrew Murray
Ben-Hur   Lew Wallace
The Christian's Secret of a Happy Life   Hannah Whitall Smith
Confessions of St. Augustine
Daily Light
Each New Day   Corrie ten Boom
Foxe's Christian Martyrs of the World
God Calling   A. J. Russell
The God of all Comfort   Hannah Whitall Smith
The Imitation of Christ   Thomas a' Kempis
In His Steps   Charles Sheldon
Mere Christianity   C. S. Lewis
The Pilgrim's Progress   John Bunyan
Purpose in Prayer/Power Through Prayer   E.M. Bounds
Quiet Talks on Prayer   S.D. Gordon

(*price may change without notice)

At Your Bookstore

Be sure to ask for Christian Library editions, in the deluxe maroo bindings.

If not available at your local bookstore, you may write to the address below. Includ $5.99 for each book you want to order, plus $2.00 for postage. Please allow two week for delivery.

Barbour and Company, Inc.
164 Mill Street
Westwood, New Jersey 07675